BURPEE AMERICAN GARDENING SERIES

SHADE GARDENING

AMERICAN GARDENING SERIES

SHADE GARDENING

Anne M. Zeman

PRENTICE HALL GARDENING

New York ◆ *London* ◆ *Toronto* ◆ *Sydney* ◆ *Tokyo* ◆ *Singapore*

For
Mark Peel
with all my love

PRENTICE HALL GENERAL REFERENCE
15 Columbus Circle
New York, NY 10023

Library of Congress Cataloging-in-Publication Data

Zeman, Anne M.
     The Burpee American gardening series. Shade gardening / Anne M.
Zeman.
         p.   cm.
     Includes index.
     ISBN 0-671-87143-9
     1. Gardening in the shade.   2. Shade-tolerant plants.   3. Shade-
tolerant plants—Pictorial works.   I. Title.   II. Title: Shade
gardening.
     SB434.7.P44   1992
     635.9′54—dc20   91-15736
                                                          CIP

Designed by Patricia Fabricant and Levavi & Levavi
Manufactured in the United States of America

10   9   8   7   6   5   4   3   2

First Edition

I am deeply grateful to Rebecca Atwater, Rachel Simon, Annie Hughes and Kim Ebert, whose superb
editorial skills and attention to detail have made this the best book possible. Special thanks to Suzanne
Bales, without whose encouragement I could not have done this book. And to Chela Kleiber, Burpee
horticulturist and Barbara Wolverton, Burpee photography coordinator, for their help and professional
thoroughness.

PHOTOGRAPHY CREDITS

Agricultural Research Services, USDA
American Daylily & Perennials
Apps, Darrel, Garden Adventures
Armitage, Dr. Allan M.
Bales, Suzanne Frutig
Cresson, Charles O.
Darke, Rick
Dirr, Michael A.
Fell, Derek
Hasselkus, E. R.
Horticultural Photography, Corvallis, Oregon

Lindtner, Peter
Oster, Maggie
PanAmerican Seed Co.
Reynolds, Kurt, Goldsmith Seeds, Inc.
Rokach, Allen
Sawyers, Claire
Still, Steven M.
Sunny Border Nurseries, Inc.
Thompson, Michael S.
Viette, Andre
Walters Gardens, Inc.

Drawings by Michael Gale
Garden Plans by Richard Gambier

On cover: *At Mohonk Mountain House, impatiens and ferns make a fail-proof combination for a shady spot*.
Preceding pages: *This wonderful woodland garden includes rare old-fashioned favorites, foxglove* (Digitalis)
behind valeriana (Centranthus ruber).

CONTENTS

Introduction

Shade is everywhere. Whether man-made or natural, it is an integral part of the landscape. All of us have some shade. Most of us don't know what to do with it.

Burpee's *Shade Gardening* was written for all gardeners who have found they can't seem to get things to grow in the shade, and it's for all of us who just want to know more about the possibilities shade plants offer. The Burpee horticulturists receive more questions about shade than almost any other subject. This book shares many of their answers.

Myths and misconceptions abound when it comes to shade. Perhaps the most common is the belief that few plants can survive in shade. In fact, there are many plants that thrive in shade, including some familiar flowering shrubs, bulbs, annuals and perennials. More than 80 plant portraits in this book provide you with a broad palette of colorful, vigorous, shade-loving plants in all shapes, sizes and textures. You'll discover there's much more to shade gardening than that old standby pachysandra.

You'll also learn about the different types of shade and how to evaluate your own shade conditions, what plants to use in partial, deep, dry and wet shade and how to solve gardening problems associated with shady areas, such as tree roots. In addition to comprehensive information on plant varieties, soil, feeding and growing methods, *Shade Gardening* provides detailed, step-by-step guidance for designing and planning your shade garden. Whether it's a woodland garden or a shady perennial bed, you'll find a wide range of colors, textures and rich foliage effects to choose from.

Once you've overcome the obstacles to growing in shade, you'll start to appreciate the unique benefits shade offers. Shade retains moisture better than full sun, so shade plants usually require less watering. Flowers hold their color and often stay in bloom longer in shade. Pests are far less common in shade, preferring sun-loving plants for their feeding frenzies.

Perhaps most important, you'll enjoy the relaxation and tranquility only a shade garden provides. The Victorians always had a cool place in the garden in which to sit and escape the sun's heat. Your shady retreat may be a terrace or deck rimmed with impatiens or clematis, a hammock stretched out beneath the arms of an old oak bordered by astilbe or cimicifuga, a trellised walkway or gazebo canopied in fragrant honeysuckle. These are the rewards of shade gardening.

The chartreuse color of lady's-mantle in the foreground shows off nicely with the gold of the small Hosta *'Gold Standard'.*

THE SHADE GARDEN PLANNER

TYPES OF SHADE

Shade, when applied to gardening, has a seemingly infinite number of definitions. For every kind and degree of shade you can imagine, there exists a term to describe it. It is important to consider degrees of shade and their effect on a certain plant in the context of existing soil conditions and the site. To simplify the problem of describing all of the various types of shade, consider the four general categories used most frequently by gardeners, nursery professionals and books and instructional guides.

1. LIGHT SHADE. An area in shade for no more than three or four hours per day. This can be an open area where a sun/shade pattern moves across the plants. Such a pattern is created by a high, thin canopy of deciduous trees, the leaves of which filter the sunlight. There is a considerable amount of direct sun, so this is a fairly bright situation. Light shade provides the greatest range of possibilities for planting because a large number of sun-loving plants will tolerate several hours of shade.

2. MEDIUM SHADE. Also known as partial shade, this is an area in shade for four to six hours per day. There is shade in the morning, or in the afternoon or intermittently throughout the day, and it is usually caused by trees or buildings obstructing what would otherwise be continuous, direct sunlight. Woodland plants and wildflowers do very well in partial shade,

as do a number of annuals and perennials. Shade-loving shrubbery such as rhododendron and azalea are more compact in growth, with more flowers.

3. FULL SHADE. An area totally shaded all day with no direct sunlight, but some indirect light. Full shade is found beneath fully leafed-out, mature trees; this more substantial shade is created by the sun-blocking canopy of such trees as oaks and maples—full and rounded, with lots of shade. Any growing area that faces North, whether it be a border or an area along a wall or fence, will be in constant shade even if it is open to the sky. A number of shade-loving shrubs such as hydrangea and rhododendron do well in full shade.

4. DENSE SHADE. This is the deepest shade of all, the sort found under a grove of evergreen trees, under shrubs, beneath decks and porches, under steps, in a dark corner and in narrow passages between houses. It has no direct sun and very little indirect light. The ground is usually dark and often dry. This is the most difficult and limiting of areas in which to plant. Some ferns and a few groundcovers will grow here but perhaps the best (and usually the quickest) solution for such dark places is to grow plants in containers. Because plants in containers can be rotated between dark and lighter spots, they broaden the range of plants for this difficult area.

The inviting shade of this garden needs only the cooling tones of green to beckon one in.

Understanding the light conditions and noting the angle of the sun as it moves over your property will help you determine the types of shade.

There are many other terms for shade. You'll often read of "open shade," "dappled shade," "morning" or "afternoon shade" and "high shade." These are all very specific kinds of shade, and it would help the gardener a great deal if specifics were used more often. Unfortunately, these terms are so specific they rarely correspond to your ideal needs. But imagine how helpful it would be when you went to your nursery or catalogs to have them describe a plant as doing well in morning sun, with afternoon shade under high, open trees. You would know exactly where to put that plant. Unfortunately, almost every plant is described as being successful in partial shade, despite the fact that the plant you are considering may do well only in the lightest of shade and would certainly die in deep shade.

Gardeners need to take some time and understand the light conditions of their property. Get to know more about the plants you have chosen for your garden. Taking time to do this early on will not only save time and effort later, but also a considerable sum of money on plants that will not survive under inhospitable conditions.

KNOW YOUR GARDEN

In order to choose from the greatest number of flowers and shrubs, you must determine the type of shade you have. You must also take note of the soil conditions as well as the site itself. In other words, you must assess your property to determine which plants will perform best for you in your particular conditions. There are a number of factors to consider: the amount and density of shade at all places on your property at all hours of the day, the trees and tree-root interference and the site and climatic conditions.

The amount and density of shade your garden receives will determine a great deal, such as how well a plant will perform. Morning sun is less strong than afternoon sun and, therefore, may be preferable for the plant you are considering. Study your locations, particularly in spring and summer, to learn where the shadows fall at different times of the day. Choose a day at various times of the year and walk your property. Trace the sun's path by checking every hour of that day. Note the angle of the sun where it hits a given area, and the amount of light or shade the area receives. Record this information by making an east-to-west diagram of the sun's journey over your property. The angle of the sun changes from season to season. In winter it rises in the southeast and sets in the southwest, but in summer it rises and sets well north of this, depending on your location.

Another consideration is the types of trees that you have and tree-root interference. Trees with tall trunks and high branches create a light shade, whereas trees with short trunks and spreading, low branches may create deeper shade. This difference in the quality of light recommends different forms of plantings. Ash, beech and silver and Norway maples all have dense foliage and shallow root systems, making it difficult for many plants to compete for nourishment. Pin oak, black locust and sycamore have lighter foliage and create less shade. Birch, honey locust and hawthorn trees have high branches and give the property below dappled sunlight; these trees are all good candidates for underplantings.

To evaluate any other trees merely dig around the base. If you have 4 to 6 inches of topsoil before reaching roots, your tree is a good candidate for underplanting.

The site and climatic conditions are also important. Evaluate the site for such basics as water availability, soil type and depth and drainage. Take note of your landscape—is it on a hill or a slope? Are there nearby streams or ponds? Does water sit after a rain? Where do the house downspouts deposit their water? You also need to know the composition of the soil. If you don't have very good soil, and most of us don't, you will need to make some improvements. (For soil improvement, see page 38.)

Shade varies with your climate. A plant that performs in full sun in high altitudes in Colorado will need considerable shade in Texas. The angle of the sun and distance your property is from the equator affect this. Prevailing winds also have an enormous effect on our climate. Most winds come from the West, but in cities that have

large buildings, or that lie along larger bodies of water, winds may come from a different direction. You may need a windbreak if you live along the ocean or along an open prairie. Westerly winds may leave a portion of your garden on the eastern side of your house unwatered, as the house may block the rain from reaching a foot or more of the plantings. The most sun will come from the south and most winds from the north and west. In shaded areas these sections will dry out the soil faster than in other places.

Getting to know your property and the different climates that surround your home will make providing the right conditions for your plants much easier.

Working with Nature

Most of us inherit the trees and plants on our property. If you have just moved into a new home you should postpone any major changes until you have lived through the various seasons. Nothing is worse than to begin digging around and tidying up only to discover later

that you had dug up peony tubers. Observe the garden and make note of plants and bloom period. Resist moving anything until you know its cultural needs. Moving a hydrangea to a more desirable location means you need to duplicate the conditions under which it is currently thriving; it may not bloom otherwise.

Trees are the foundation of every property. They provide shade for our homes as well as our gardens. They give us shelter and privacy. They provide homes for the birds and squirrels, and help the environment by changing atmospheric carbon dioxide into oxygen. With higher-branching trees (oak and birch, for example) and wider spacing of trees, the overhead canopy turns the understory from deep, to full or even medium shade. The large shade trees that allow for the most successful underplanting, in addition to those mentioned above, are the red, black and white oak (least wanted is the pin oak); sugar maple; honey locust; yellowwood and elm.

There are a number of small ornamental trees that work quite

Above left: *This variegated* Hydrangea *is a bright welcome to this very private, shady retreat.*

Above right: *A collection of ferns, hostas and epimediums makes a lush underplanting.*

well in the garden, deep-rooted so that plants can flourish beneath them. Small trees are preferable for small gardens and can be grown close to foundations, terraces and pavement. The flowering cherry and crab apple are all pretty choices as are hawthorn and the exotic goldenrain tree.

All trees have roots that compete to some degree with the underplanting. However, deep-rooted trees usually have enough surface area where other plants can survive without competing for nutrition and moisture. The aforementioned trees are deep rooted and, therefore, preferable. Trees such as European beech and most maples create shade that is too dense for underplantings, and they also have very fibrous root systems, which are too competitive for smaller plants. The horse chestnut and the white pine also have thick root systems and should be avoided. Norway maple is a notorious thug—once large and established, it is seldom that anything grows under this tree.

This striking, variegated Euonymus *is attractive and easy to grow in nearly every part of North America.*

Ivy, pachysandra, periwinkle and moneywort are groundcovers that may oblige with periodic encouragement of nutrients and fertilizers.

There are several things to keep in mind when selecting a tree. First and foremost is tolerance to soil conditions and compatability with other plants that will be growing under or near it. Next consider its habit of foliage and mature spread, depth of root system, ornamental interest, structural strength, disease resistance, litter problem and recovery time from movement and transplanting. One of the biggest mistakes first-time gardeners make is planting too close together. When you plant a tree, be sure to find out what the spread will be when mature and plant accordingly. Planting too close results in overcrowding. Taking the time to plan well will avoid the need to move the tree later.

Pruning for More Light

A mature low-branching tree will cast dense shade over the area beneath it, limiting the selection of plants that will grow beneath it. These growing conditions can be modified so the gardener can make use of the ground beneath the branches. Branches can be pruned to allow more light to pass through them. This can be done by thinning the principal branches so the tree has less foliage. Thinning out the dense foliage of leaves can also improve the air circulation under the tree, and good air circulation is essential to the health of plants. This is especially true for shade plants that receive little, if any, direct sun and need the air circulation to keep their foliage dry. Shade-loving shrubs will benefit from thinning too.

In addition to thinning, you can also raise the canopy farther from the ground by pruning the lower branches of the tree. Pruning these lower branches can permit sun in on just one or several sides, depending on the severity of the pruning. Take note of the sun's pattern and prune according to the shadows the tree casts on the ground where you want to put your plants. Perhaps only one branch need be pruned to give you the light necessary for the flower bed beneath. A neighbor of mine keeps his oak trees pruned to 40 feet up the tree. This allows him to have some light at all areas under the tree, with no area in deep shade.

The pruning of mature trees is probably best left to the tree surgeons, professionals experienced at working at dangerous heights. There are real safety concerns for the inexperienced. For younger or smaller trees you may wish to do your own pruning. Never prune more than one-third of the branches in any year. After severe pruning there is usually a spurt of growth that can make the tree even more dense, and possibly even choke it. Pruning is usually done in the winter, but if you plan to prune heavily, it is best to do so in late June or July, when the tree is at the time of fullest growth and the cut will be partially covered with new bark before the plant stops growing in early fall.

Minimizing Root Competition

The shallow root systems of the maple and beech are the curse of the shade gardener. Too many roots not only make digging difficult, but cause problems for smaller plants trying to compete for nutrients and moisture. Usually these smaller plants can't compete and expire. Short of replacing the shallow-rooted tree with a deep-rooted tree, there is not too much that can be done. The best solution is to plant a groundcover that needs relatively little water and nourishment—ivy, for example.

It is possible to remove a single, large root and its feeder roots close to the surface without damaging the tree in order to create a small planting bed. This must be done carefully by choosing a partially exposed root near the trunk. Use a hatchet to remove the root and dislodge it from the soil approximately 4 feet out from the tree and 2 feet deep. Use fresh topsoil with lots of organic matter to fill in the new bed. This bed, too, will have to be maintained every year or two to keep the roots from invading again. As you improve the soil for the new plants you also encourage and feed the tree roots.

One thing you mustn't do is add a heavy extra layer of soil on top of what is already in place. You may kill the tree, or the new soil may be invaded by the tree roots within a season in their search for nutrients. Take the precautions as described above or plant a groundcover. Some people prefer to remove the tree altogether to open up the area for a new bed or border.

PLANTS FOR DEEP SHADE UNDER TREES

Bulbs (many varieties, including *Scilla*, snowdrops and wood hyacinth)
Convallaria
Epimedium
Ferns
Hedera species (ivy)
Hosta species
Mertensia
Pachysandra
Polygonatum species
Vinca minor

TREES WITH SHALLOW ROOT SYSTEMS, DIFFICULT FOR UNDERPLANTING

Beech
Black walnut (poisonous roots)
Norway maple
Pin oak
Red maple
Silver maple
Sycamore

TREES GOOD FOR UNDERPLANTING

Birch
Black oak
Cherry
Crab apple
Hawthorn
Honey locust
Red oak
White oak
Yellowwood

COLOR IN THE SHADE GARDEN

When we think of shady areas most of us don't think of flowers, but there are a number of shade-loving plants that bloom very well indeed without the benefit of full sun. There are hundreds of flowers that tolerate partial shade and many that even prefer shade. It's not that difficult to find flowers that grow in the sun, but the challenge is to stop trying to grow plants that prefer sun and begin growing plants that are happy in shade. This chapter will give you information about choice color plants for the shade by season.

BULBS FOR SPRING COLOR

The most welcome sight of all is that of the first color of the season, spring bulbs popping their heads up to announce spring. Most of the spring bulbs do need a fair amount of sun, but the majority of the time they get all that is necessary before the deciduous trees leaf-out to create shade. If you have light during winter and spring under high trees or beside buildings that have good reflected light, you can grow spring bulbs. They are not for planting under evergreen or shallow-rooted trees such as Norway maple.

These early heralds of spring are snowdrops (*Galanthus*), crocus and winter aconite (*Eranthis hyemalis*). These are the earliest of the spring bulbs and begin to bloom in February and March in most areas. By midspring the windflowers (*Anemone*) have opened their daisylike blooms along with the dogtooth violet (*Erythronium*), whose lilac or yellow flowers are sometimes mistaken for lilies. The early iris (*Iris reticulata*) grows only 5 inches tall and is a delightful spring flower. The daffodils (*Narcissus*) appear sequentially depending on the variety. The yellow trumpet forms bloom first, followed by the large-cupped and then the double varieties. 'King Alfred' is America's best-known daffodil but there are many other varieties that have been improved upon. (See the plant portraits for recommended varieties of daffodils.)

The squill (*Scilla*) is hardy and indispensable. The Siberian squill 'Spring Beauty' is an improved variety and is one of the bluest of flowers. It also is one of the few bulbs that thrives under evergreens. The wood hyacinth (*Scilla campanulata*) is one of the latest spring bulbs to flower.

The same rules about light requirements can be applied to tulips. I grow every kind of tulip in those areas that receive the light before the trees leaf-out. The earliest-blooming of all tulip varieties are the Kaufmanniana, and they come up before most deciduous trees have their leaves. The same holds true for the single and double early varieties. I grow the double late varieties in partial shade and have had very good performance. Take note of the times when your trees leaf-out and plant tulips accordingly.

Ferns, impatiens and fuschias make a colorful combination for shade.

SPRING WOODLAND FAVORITES

Choice Primroses

There has never been a more charming and irresistible flower than the primrose. Shakespeare immortalized it in *Hamlet* and the Victorians created paths and paths of them in their turn-of-the-century gardens. Primroses are among the favorites of the flowering perennials for shady areas. Their colors are bright, boisterous and cheerful and their flowers pop up in little, ready-made bouquets. They are perfect for the woodland setting, lining paths or beside a pool or brook. Plant them by a path shaded by rhododendron or other shrubs, under an evergreen and in crooked paths under high trees. Primroses do best in medium shade with some intermittent sun for a short part of the day. Under no circumstances do they like noon sun and they prefer an eastern or northern exposure. A primrose path is irresistibly tempting to follow, so be sure to plant lots of them. Plant primroses early and they will supply you with wonderful bouquets of color all spring.

The cherry red and gold colors of primroses and the rosy pink of this deciduous azalea are perennial springtime favorites.

One of the earliest primroses is *Primula denticulata* and it's one of the easiest to grow. For bright, cheerful color try the Pacific Giants type, *P.* ×*polyantha* 'Dwarf-Jewel'. These are the "bunch primroses," perhaps the most popular primrose of all. *P. vulgaris* is the beloved English primrose acknowledged by Shakespeare and Keats, among others, but it is not easy to find. These are all varieties no shade garden should be without.

The Sweetest Violets

One of the most old-fashioned and romantic of flowers, the violet has been chronicled in legends of the ancient gods as well as by Homer, who described sweet-smelling violets in *The Odyssey*. The violet was the emblem of ancient Athens and later adopted by the old city of Parma, Italy, which became famous for its Parma violet perfume. The beauty and fragrance of violets have been the inspiration for many a poem, and its dainty, fragrant flowers are one of the first signs of spring.

Violets and pansies belong to the same family. Violets have smaller flowers than pansies, but violets bloom longer on neater plants. Easily grown and dependable, violets will bloom from early spring until frost (if not overheated and if faded blossoms are picked regularly). They are lovely in beds, rock gardens and as edgings. In the South and Pacific Southwest they are grown for winter bloom. They are easy to grow in shady, cool spots. Violets are spreading plants, so give them plenty of room. For this reason they are good for naturalizing and can provide a charming groundcover.

Not all violets are scented but the queen of the scented violets is the *Viola odorata*. One of my favorite violets is *V. pedata* (bird's-foot violet), a native to eastern and midwestern America, with lovely lilac flowers that will do well even in sun (except for in the warmest regions of the country). Also try white varieties, especially *Viola* 'White Czar', which creeps over the garden like a shimmering blanket. The *V. tricolor hortensis*, also known as Johnny-jump-ups, are an old-fashioned favorite and one of the happiest-looking pansies you'll ever meet. Violets and pansies combine nicely with spring bulbs and primroses.

Additional Woodland Flowers

The shadiest part of your property can be turned into a walk through a garden of woodland plants and wildflowers. Early in spring before the canopy of trees fills in, there is an enticing number of flowering plants that bloom. These woodland plants and wildflowers are sometimes called the "spring ephemerals" because they simply disappear as the trees leaf-out. These are among the most treasured of plants and many are our own Native American plants.

One of the most popular of all the woodland wildflowers is the trillium. *Trillium grandiflorum* has handsome white flowers that last up to a month and are easy to grow. Often in the wild you will see lady's slipper (*Cypripedium*) lifting its head above a sea of trillium, but lady's slipper needs a particular fungus to survive and, therefore, is difficult. Plants should never be taken from the wild.

Other widely available woodland plants are bloodroot (*Sanguinaria*), bleeding heart (*Dicentra*), foamflower (*Tiarella*) and Virginia bluebells (*Mertensia*) in addition to primrose and violet. If your garden has moist shade try marsh marigold or the cardinal flower (*Lobelia*

Cardinalis). Jack-in-the-pulpit (*Arisaema*) is excellent for boggy areas, but again, this is a difficult plant to reestablish and should not be taken from the wild; seeds are now available from reputable nurseries.

Winter aconite (Eranthis hyemalis) and snowdrops (Galanthus nivalis) are naturalized in this woodland.

EASY SUMMER BULBS

The lily (*Lilium*) is the summer bulb of choice. Lilies rank among the finest garden plants, providing exquisite form, glorious color and delightful fragrance. Because vigor and disease resistance are bred into the hybrid lily bulbs, you will enjoy their beauty for years. One of the oldest cultivated flowers, the lily has been cherished since before the time of Christ. As a popular flower in ancient Jewish civilization, the lily is frequently mentioned in the Old Testament. The lily became associated with the Virgin Mary and so the Madonna lily (*L. candidum*) became a symbol of purity, as well as one of the most popular lilies of all time.

Few plants are as versatile and easy as the lily. There are almost 100 species of lilies to choose from and they come in all sizes, forms, colors and heights. Most are fragrant. Their growing conditions vary but, once established, they increase in beauty year after year; some varieties may die out after three years. Major breakthroughs by breeders have been made in the last few decades that have resulted in greater adaptability, vigor and color range, giving us great new additions to the home gardener.

Asiatic hybrids, named for

their Asian ancestors, are elegant lilies that bloom in June and July. They are easy to grow and multiply quickly. They flourish in light and medium shade. The Asiatics are the most widely varied group in color and form and are usually the hardiest. They have a long bloom time and are excellent cut flowers.

Commonly known as "trumpet" lilies, the regal Aurelian hybrids reign in stately elegance over the midsummer garden. These lilies are generally taller than the Asiatics and bloom later. Their height gives them special usefulness at the back of the perennial border, where they add vertical interest and visual depth. The perfume of trumpet lilies reaches every corner of the garden and is always pleasant, never cloying. They are very long lasting as cut flowers and make spectacular arrangements. They retain their color and vigor better if they receive just a half day of sun, preferably in the morning.

Species lilies are the oldest of the lilies and have been treasured by generations of gardeners. They have a particular charm and grace all their own. They include the Madonna lily (*L. candidum*) and the regal lily (*L. regale*). The Madonna lily is

a classic beauty with a sweet fragrance. Stately 3- to 4-foot stalks bear clusters of pure white blooms, a glorious sight in any garden. It flowers in June and looks wonderful with blue delphinium.

The regal lily could not be more appropriately named because it is majestic in every way. This classic lily is one of the parents of the Aurelian hybrids. Once established it will produce as many as 20 blooms on 4-foot stems in early summer. The trumpets are snowy white with yellow throats and lilac-pink exteriors and are delightfully fragrant.

The cultivation of lilies is not difficult. Their first requirement is excellent drainage. They need a light but substantial soil, not heavy, clay or sandy. Most species need an acid soil, with the exception of *L. candidum* and *L. chalcedonicum*, which prefer a heavy, alkaline soil. Exposure to excessive heat and winds can be harmful, and too much shade can result in fewer blooms. Their bulbs and roots should be well shaded; use a ground cover or a low-growing perennial.

Daylilies

Not to be confused with the lilies, the flower commonly called

A naturalized mixture of daylilies.

daylily is in the genus *Hemerocallis*. *Hemerocallis* is not a bulb, has no foliage along the stem, and has longer leaves. Their wonderful blooms are perfect for a day and gone the next. They are versatile, offer a rainbow of colors and come in a variety of heights, forms and sizes. They multiply generously yet do not overrun their neighbors.

There are so many daylilies being developed by breeders that almost 30,000 named daylily cultivars are listed with the American Hemerocallis Society. The old-fashioned daylily (*H. fulva*), the one you see alongside the roads across the country, has been improved on to such a degree that there is a greater profusion of blooms that can last a month or longer. Depending on where you live, and utilizing different cultivars, you can plan for a succession of blooms from June until October. The bloom season is divided into early (late May and June), middle (late June and July) and late (August and September).

In addition to a profusion of bloom, daylily foliage is attractive for most, if not all, of the growing season. Their leaves emerge in pairs from an underground stem and open like a fan, making a handsome, fountainlike clump. They appear in April and can hide the yellowing leaves of daffodils and tulips in late spring. Daylilies are stunning in a bed using repeating colors and your favorite mixtures. Try them in the mixed border or to highlight either end of a hosta or fern planting.

Caladium

Caladiums are luxuriant plants of a tropical nature that will light up any shady area. They are grown for their large, broad, arrowhead- or heart-shaped leaves tinted with shades of green, silver, white or rose. These beautifully veined and variegated plants produce masses of lush color throughout the entire summer right up until frost. They are used extensively in the southern states because they thrive in summer heat.

There are fancy-leafed and lance-leafed caladiums. The only difference between the two is the shape of the leaf—fancy-leafed are more heart-shaped; lance-leafed, more arrow-shaped. They are very easy to grow and are ideal for containers. There is a great array of colors and patterns from which to choose. Caladiums make a strong visual element along paths, in the border or by themselves in a single bed. Most mail-order catalogs offer selections in mixed colors. Should you be tempted to try several different colors in one spot, resist the urge; they almost always clash. When combining even two kinds it takes planning and experimentation. Planting masses of a single variety is the safe method. Use a dozen or more together to provide a mass of color throughout summer and fall.

Collections of Caladium *make a bright showing in shady spots.*

CAREFREE ANNUALS

Annuals are the easiest and quickest way to provide glorious color in the shade garden. Annuals are the flowers that complete their life cycle in a single season. They are prolific bloomers, come in a multitude of colors, and will tolerate most kinds of soil. They are a good introduction to gardening for the beginner, and an inexpensive one at that.

Annuals are a blessing to summer flower beds. Blooming from spring until frost, they can be massed in the border or mixed with perennials and bulbs. Use them for filling in gaps while young perennials are becoming established. Try drifts by the doorway or along the terrace—anywhere you'd like a splash of color in your shady spots. The two most popular shade-garden annuals are impatiens and begonias. They are popular for a good reason: They provide spectacular splashes of color in all kinds of shade.

Impatiens

Impatiens are among the most dependable of all flowering annuals. Nothing can beat them for brilliant, summer-to-fall bloom in shady beds, borders and containers. They are easy to start from seed and are readily available from every nursery. The 'Rosette' hybrid is a mixture of doubles and semidoubles that look like miniature roses. Another outstanding impatiens is the New Guinea impatiens, some of which have variegated leaves and look so especially nice in those darker spots. Impatiens make outstanding potted plants, and if you live in a frost-free area they thrive outdoors all year.

Impatiens can be massed beautifully along the drive or walkway, and combine nicely with other shade-growing plants. A mass planting of impatiens can be a spectacular sight to behold.

Ever-blooming Begonias

Begonias manage in almost all light conditions but they do best in light shade. They bloom continuously all summer until frost, adapt beautifully to bedding or edging and are ideal for window boxes and containers. They provide brilliant color with shades of pink, rose, red and white and foliage either green or bronze.

There are tuberous begonias and wax begonias. Wax begonias are low-growing and ever-blooming. Begonias are tender perennials, so in the North they are grown as annuals. They may be grown outdoors in summer and moved indoors before the first frost.

Tuberous begonias are elegant summer flowers. Their flowers may be single or double and their foliage is velvety, crinkled and prettier than that of other begonias. They grow best where summer temperatures are relatively cool and for this reason do not perform as well in the south. You can grow them in the ground or in pots, but they must be dug up and replanted each year because they will not survive the cold. For this reason I usually grow them in pots and move them indoors in fall. For additional information on tuberous and wax begonias see "Plant Portraits."

Nicotiana

Nicotiana is the flowering tobacco plant, a relative of the N. Tabacum, whose leaves are used for smoking. This easy annual does extremely well in light and medium shade and is a prolific bloomer. Several varieties are quite fragrant.

The whole house will be fragrant from one bouquet of N. alata or N. sylvestris, the old-fashioned varieties of Nicotiana. These delightful plants are not readily available from nurseries but you can usually find them in seed catalogs. It is definitely worth the effort of sending for them. They grow 2 to 3½ feet, with tubular flowers that open with an intoxicating scent. If grown in the sun, their flowers remain closed all day—they open in the shade. For evening

scent they must be grown en masse for the best effects of the fragrance and to provide a steady supply for the house. Grow them near the porch or terrace to fully appreciate them on summer evenings. An added attraction for those two varieties is that they attract beautiful nocturnal moths.

The one disadvantage to the old-fashioned varieties is that they usually need to be staked. For this reason dwarf versions became more popular, and there are some very good varieties. The N. alata 'Nicki Hybrids' are an attractive, versatile, semidwarf variety with an old-fashioned look. They have wonderful color and long bloom, but little fragrance. The Domino Series and the Sensation Series are also good.

Flowering tobaccos are perennials in the South. As annuals they will sometimes reseed themselves. All the varieties are useful for growing in mass plantings and as vertical accents when combined with annuals that have a trailing habit.

Pansies

Pansies are the annual variety of the Viola. They are treasured for their bright colors and as sweet-faced companions of

Hosta 'Royal Standard' coupled with pink and white impatiens make a glowing boundary planting.

Ever-blooming begonias and Nicotiana *are colorful all season long.*

spring-flowering bulbs. New hybrid varieties are bred for extra vigor and heat tolerance. Pansies are no longer a spring-blooming flower only; some varieties will bloom well into—and on occasion all through—summer.

Viola tricolor, better known as the Johnny-jump-up, is one of the all-time favorite pansies. It's a smaller plant with little flowers in solid, bicolors or picotees (edged with a different color) that bloom from early spring to frost. There are numerous modern hybrids and the following are some of the best:

SWISS GIANTS. Exceptional vigor with enormous flowers up to 3 inches in diameter, with velvety texture in a compact habit. Wide range of colors. Blooms early spring to midsummer.

MAJESTIC GIANTS. An All-American Winner. Extremely large flowers up to 4 inches across with handsome, medium-size faces on long stems good for cutting. Heat tolerant.

JUMBO GIANTS. Early flowering and remaining in bloom to frost, sometimes up to six months. Good color combinations.

There are three other single hybrids that have won the All-American Winner award: 'Imperial Blue', an excellent pansy with large, light blue flowers and bluish violet faces, 'Orange Prince', apricot-orange blossoms with deep mahogany faces, and 'Padparadja', a 1991 AAS Winner, 2-inch-deep orange flowers named after the orange sapphire from Sri Lanka.

Plant pansies in any area that has partial shade. They thrive in fairly rich, well-drained soil. Keep faded flowers picked and plants pinched back to encourage new growth and you will be rewarded with bright, cheery colors all spring and summer.

PERENNIALS FOR COLOR

There is a multitude of perennials for the shade with endless color combinations to choose from. Use these flowering plants to brighten a shady area, surround your terrace or to change the ambiance of the garden.

Among the first to bloom are the old-fashioned bleeding hearts (*Dicentra*). The name comes from the heart shape of the flower. Gardeners have treasured them for centuries for their lovely, pendant, heart-shaped flowers, borne on gracefully arching branches. Their foliage is intricately divided, resembling airy maidenhair ferns. *Dicentra spectabilis* is the showy, old-fashioned favorite. Try *D. spectabilis* 'Alba', a white variety that is especially effective in evening light. Bleeding hearts are perfect companions for hosta.

Digitalis, commonly known as foxglove, is one of the oldest favorites in the American garden. It is not really a perennial but rather a biennial; that is, it produces foliage the first year and flowers the second, completing the cycle. They usually reseed themselves each flowering year, enabling the gardener to have a continuous showing of plants. *Digitalis* are charming plants that grow in spikes nearly 2 feet high. The flowers are large and bell-shaped, arranged in very long racemes (unbranched flower clusters) that resemble thimbles. This is an excellent plant for the hardy border, giving an appearance of strength in addition to its beauty.

Digitalis purpurea, the common garden foxglove, is the biennial that is the most spectacular in the garden. Its spikes of purple-speckled flowers bloom in early summer, and it frequently self-sows. There is a strain called Foxy that blooms in the first year as well as the second. The Shirley and Excelsior Hybrids are quite exceptional in that they have large and showy flowers. The *Digitalis × mertonensis* is the perennial foxglove that comes in the most beautiful shade of rose. Most perennial foxgloves are short-lived and must be divided every two to three years.

It's impossible to talk about perennials for the shade without mentioning *Astilbe*. *Astilbe* is an excellent choice for a shady, moist area. It is a premium plant for medium and full shade, and will occasionally even tolerate deep shade. It is grown for both its foliage and its flowers. Its showy, featherlike plumes bloom in shades of red, pink and white in early to midsummer. The foliage is gracefully cut, almost fernlike, and displays rich tones of green and bronze—handsome all season long. The 2-foot plant is easy to grow, thrives on moisture and increases in beauty year after year.

Astilbe works very well as a

Few plants can rival the grace and charm of feathery Astilbe.

potted plant. Its spikes are wonderful as long-lasting cut flowers fresh, pretty when dried too. When bringing them in for fresh-flower arrangements, be sure to harvest them when the blossoms are half open: they will last much longer. *Astilbe* is a long-lived perennial. Its greatest enemy is dryness. Never let it dry out. For this reason it is not well suited to excessively hot and dry climates, unless at a high altitude.

Aquilegia is known widely by its common name columbine. It is one of the most beloved of old-fashioned garden plants and one of the best for shade. Many species are native to eastern America and are usually found in shady, moist areas. Columbine strongly appeals to the imagination because of the unusually fanciful shape of its flowers and leaves. The flowers are double corollas with petals widening into a horn shape, which lengthens into long spurs. Its leaves are delicately notched, airy and elegant looking, in shades of green and blue-green.

There are few spots in the shady garden to which some form of columbine is not appropriate.

It is perfect for the perennial border, woodland path or cutting garden. Columbine is available in a multitude of colors and makes an elegant addition to your late-spring and early-summer garden. It combines nicely with ferns; an added advantage to planting with ferns is that they hide the fading columbine foliage after flowering.

An unusual plant for light shade is lady's-mantle (*Alchemilla*). It has silvery, scalloped leaves topped by airy clusters of chartreuse summer flowers. Eighteen inches high and absolutely weedproof, the lady's-mantle is best in a slightly damp place. In addition to its wonderful yellow-green color, it is quite vigorous and can be downright invasive. It's a wonderful controller of excess space, but if you don't want it to get out of hand simply cut the plant back after flowering, before its seeds throw themselves everywhere. They bloom in July and August and are good cut flowers. Combine them with a purple-leafed plant for an interesting combination.

Another unusual and striking perennial for the shade is the common bugbane (*Cimicifuga racemosa*). It's also called "fairy candle" and, indeed, the flowers look like them in shady corners, with their tall, elegant spikes of white flowers towering 3 to 4 feet high. It blooms late summer and early fall when many other flowers have faded.

Cranesbill is the true hardy geranium and is good for any ordinary soil, even in dry shade. The *Geranium Endressii* forms a nice clump and works as a companion plant under and in front of shrubs. The Wargrave cultivars are also fine. Try 'Johnson's Blue' for its vivid blue color. These really can't be beat for color in dry shade.

The colorful, flowering favorites of rosebud azalea, columbine, bleeding heart and foxglove line this woodland walk.

SHADY SHRUBS

Deciduous, broad-leafed and needle-leafed evergreens—within these classifications, there is no end to the diversity of shrubs or limit to their usefulness. Shrubs form the backbone of your garden. They are the unifying element that blends your plantings into one harmonious landscape. Shrubs define spaces or screen views, soften the lines of buildings and tie them into the landscape or create architectural interest. They provide the ideal background for annual

or perennial borders, and many provide fall and winter food for birds. The selection of shrubs listed here all perform well in the shade, and are known for their superb garden performance and ease of culture.

The family of the viburnums offers a first-class plant for almost any place. Use it anywhere for its scent and its long season of attractive leaves, berries and white flowers. *Viburnum Carlesii*, the Korean spicebush, has no equal in fragrance. It is not

the quickest grower, but it has the strongest scent of any of the viburnums. It's an early bloomer, flowering at the same time as tulips. The spectacular flower clusters are followed by black berries. It is parent to a number of other viburnums such as the *V. × Juddii*, one of the best for the northern regions. *V. × Juddii* was developed at the Arnold Arboretum in Boston specifically to withstand severe cold. It too has fragrant flowers, and produces reddish black fruit. A choice shrub for the South is *V. ×Burkwoodii* because its shiny green foliage remains evergreen. If you enjoy the birds, be sure to choose a viburnum that produces berries after it flowers.

There are viburnums known as the Japanese snowballs. These feature large, ball-shaped clusters that bear sterile, white flowers in late spring. Most of these viburnums do not produce berries. The most commonly found snowball viburnum is the *V. Opulus* 'Sterile' and the one probably to be found in your grandmother's garden. One of the loveliest viburnums is Marie's double file viburnum (*V. plicatum tomentosum* 'Mariesii'). It bears a cluster of fertile flowers surrounded by sterile flowers on the outside. It grows to almost 10 feet and produces 2- to 4-inch blooms as well as red berries that mature to black and last well into autumn. Take a look at them, because viburnums are an excellent choice for the shade garden.

Viburnums for the Birds

Birds will eat the berries of any berry-producing viburnum. Note whether the plant you are about to purchase produces fruit. Here are a few of the birds' favorites:

V. dentatum (arrowwood)

V. dilatatum (linden viburnum)

V. Opulus (European cranberry bush)

V. plicatum tomentosum 'Mariesii' (Marie's double file viburnum)

V. setigerum 'Aurantiacum' (orange-fruited viburnum)

V. Sieboldii (Siebold's viburnum)

V. trilobum (American cranberry bush)

The early spring season also brings along the mountain laurel (*Kalmia*), andromeda (*Pieris*) and *Fothergilla*. The site of a woodland hillside of blooming mountain laurels is stunning. A North American native, it is evergreen and one of the overall best broad-leafed plants for the garden. It makes an ideal foundation planting as it is well formed, hardy and long lived. This beautiful evergreen shrub is appreciated everywhere and has been named the state flower of Connecticut and Pennsylvania.

Another early spring bloomer is andromeda (*Pieris*). This is a splendid shrub, a long-time favorite that produces most unusual, drooping flower panicles in April and May. The hardiest are the *P. floribunda* and *P. japonica*. Look for the new red varieties coming onto the market. Recently I saw a *P. japonica* 'Variegata' that had striking, red-tinted new growth and mature leaves that were variegated and quite interesting.

Just after the andromeda flowers the *Fothergilla Gardenii* comes into bloom. This rare and choice dwarf shrub produces creamy white flowers that smell like honey in May, but its main attraction is the brilliant yellow and orange fall foliage color. It is invaluable in the small garden and also works well with azalea and rhododendron.

Gardens of viburnum, mountain laurel and andromeda are weighted toward the early part of the season. Balance them with hydrangea for the latter part of the growing season. Hydrangea is among the most spectacular of summer- and autumn-flowering shrubs. It performs beautifully in all types of shade, under trees or to the north side of a house. There are basically two kinds of hydrangea: the large flower-headed type and the lace-cap variety. The best-known and most popular are the ones with the large flower heads, *Hydrangea macrophylla*. They have large balloonlike flowers that are reminiscent of the snowball bushes. The English have a wonderful term for them: the *mopheads*. Their flower balls sometimes get so large they do look like mopheads hanging from the bush. The lace-caps are quite different. Each flat flower head has an outer ring of large flowers surrounding a central group of smaller flowers. They have a much daintier look to them.

Hydrangea is not difficult but you must satisfy its voracious appetite for food and water. Hydrangea should never be allowed to be dry during the summer; this is ruinous. Sometimes the leaves will get wrinkled and your immediate reaction will be to suspect a bug, but water first and the plant will usually return to normal. This shrub needs a heavy top-dressing of well-rotted manure and an annual dose of slow-release fertilizer in early spring. The tendency will be to keep feeding from July onward to encourage more growth while their buds are forming, but this only encourages new growth until late fall, when it will be hit by frost. Feed it in early spring and early summer, but no later. This will help you keep your hydrangea at its best for years.

The color of your hydrangea depends on the acidity of the

soil. Blue flowers are produced in an acid soil. Many people marvel at the blue hydrangea that grew to be pink the following year. A dressing of iron sulfate will keep your flowers blue, or you can add leaf mold, lime, peat moss or another type of acidic material if you prefer.

In addition to these marvelous hydrangea shrubs, there is also an excellent climbing hydrangea, *H. anomala petiolaris*. There may not be a better climbing vine. This climbs walls and tree trunks by means of aerial roots, and it requires no additional supports. It has creamy white flowers that bloom in June and July and is very hardy. Sometimes it is slow to become established, but once it starts, it grows well each year.

Rhododendron and Azalea

Rhododendron and azalea are probably the most popular shrubs in America. Practically every home has at least one, and a drive through many neighborhoods will show you dozens of varieties. Botanically, azalea is part of the *Rhododendron* genus. Both rhododendron and azalea are superb landscaping plants with handsome foliage (often evergreen) and striking flowers. They can be found in all sizes and colors except for a true blue. They are excellent foundation plantings, for naturalizing in drifts in an open woodland setting and for planting in groups throughout the landscape. One of the most spectacular displays of rhododendron and azalea is at the National Arboretum in Washington,

D.C., where slopes and hillsides are bathed in glorious springtime color.

Rhododendron and azalea require little care. All require a shady position and some shelter. They are shallow rooted and should be planted carefully as recommended—not too deep. Due to their shallow roots the surface ground around them should not be stirred or cultivated. Digging among the roots can be destructive and should be avoided. A plentiful supply of moisture is needed and a thorough soaking should be done on a weekly basis in dry weather.

Rhododendron usually doesn't need fertilizing as long as there is healthy growth. Older plants or plants that are not producing healthy growth benefit by an annual application of well-rotted manure in early spring. Azalea, on the other hand, needs regular fertilizing each year. Use well-rotted manure, cottonseed meal, soybean meal or a prepared mixture especially for acid-loving plants.

A cool, moist, acid soil (pH 4.5 to 6.5) is needed with good drainage and a high percentage of organic matter to retain moisture. Use a mulch 2 to 3 inches deep to protect the roots from excessive heat in summer and excessive cold in winter. The mulch will also help retain moisture and keep the weeds to a minimum, thus eliminating the need to cultivate and cause possible harm to the roots. Wood chips, hardwood sawdust, pine needles and well-rotted manure are all good mulches.

Azalea and rhododendron need little pruning. Most need merely a good grooming to

retain shape. When pruning, always do so after flowering. A young rhododendron can become leggy and should be cut back to encourage a bushy habit. If you have an old plant that has grown tall and leggy a drastic pruning may be done in spring before new growth begins. Cut the bush down to about 1 foot above the ground and fertilize and mulch. This will encourage new growth and the more preferred shape. Be prepared for the shrub not to be in bloom for 2 to 3 years following this drastic pruning, but the results will be worth the wait.

Faded flowers should be removed from rhododendron and azalea. This will avoid the development of seedpods, so the plant can save energy for the next year's growth. (You may want to leave a few seedpods on if you want to yield seeds for propagation purposes, but those flower buds may not develop for next year's bloom.)

Top: *The lace-cap hydrangea has spectacular blooms in late summer and fall.*

Above: *Rhododendron and azalea create a glorious setting.*

DESIGNING THE SHADE GARDEN

Designing your garden is one of the most important things you will do as a gardener. Unfortunately it is the area that many people find the most intimidating. It can seem complicated, and people sometimes feel they need the help of a professional. But it really isn't that difficult if you just handle some basic preparation ahead of time. All you really need is a mixture of good taste, a lot of common sense and a reasonable understanding of the principles of design.

GETTING A GENERAL VIEW

Before we jump into design, first take a broad view of your property. You need to get to know your property. Chapter 1 outlined how to note your topographical features, the climate, the sun's path and existing trees and plants. Take your surveyor's map of your property and walk every boundary. Find out where the underground service lines are—the sewer lines or septic tank, water pipes, gas lines, underground electric cables and so on. This information is important if you plan to do any digging or use a Rototiller. Next note the views. Look at your house in relation to everything that is around it. The house dominates the small home landscape and it is a common mistake to overlook it. Look for any obtrusive objects that may need to be screened out. And don't forget the neighbor's lot— you may need a screen or a hedge for privacy, or something as simple as a small shrub to hide their garbage pails that you can see from your kitchen. In addition to viewing your property from the outside, view it from the inside. Look out your windows and note the views from each of the rooms. Do you want something bright and cheery to enjoy from the kitchen, something more formal from the living room or bedroom? This, too, will affect how you plan your design.

In this general survey you also need to consider whoever might be sharing this landscape with you. If there are small children, you may want a play area with a sand box and a swing set. Adults and teenagers may want an entertainment area such as a terrace. Dogs and other pets may need a running area or shelter. If you want an area for a vegetable garden or a cutting garden, this needs to be taken into consideration. Noting the needs of your lifestyle will help you make your plan the best design for *living* use.

Plan on Paper

Once you have considered the broad view and have taken a hard look at your grounds, make a map of your place. This seems like the difficult part to many, but it's not difficult at all. Your sketch need not be professional looking, but it needs to be made to scale. Use a scale ruler for

Heuchera 'Purple Palace' and *Lamium 'Beacon Silver' make a wonderful combination.*

translating feet into inches if you like. I find it easier to use either ¼ inch or ½ inch to the foot depending on the size of the property. It is usually easier to work with ½ inch—fine for smaller properties. Graph paper is the ideal way to lay out your plan and you can use each square on the paper to represent a foot as well; this way you need only to count the squares as you make your plan.

You will need to measure your entire property and this should be done when you walk your boundaries. Start with the outside perimeters and work in.

When you moved to your property you probably had a survey done, and you can use this surveyor's map for your plan if you use the same scale. You can also use this to trace relevant buildings onto your plan. After the boundaries, measure the house, garage and any other buildings. Next come the trees, shrubs, walls, large rocks, paths and ornaments. Draw these on the map.

You have now created the "skeleton" of your property. This will permit you to see the property as a unit, making relationships of parts to the whole more easy to grasp. You are now

ready to start filling in all the features you want to add. I find it helpful to make many copies of this skeletal plan, to try different ideas. Make as many rough sketches as needed until you get your plan exactly the way you want it, but make all of your mistakes on paper. Trying, discarding and changing on paper instead of directly in your garden will give you better results than trial and error in the garden. If you've ever tried to move a tree, you know it's a lot easier to move it on paper than after it's established in your backyard.

PRINCIPLES OF GARDEN DESIGN

This self-contained garden features fuschias and impatiens, all surrounded by ivy that has been clipped to form a design on the wall.

Each part of your property will represent a different kind of design challenge. The area outside the kitchen door will call for different solutions than the woodland path at the far end of the property. Each area should be a balanced composition in relation to the unified whole. Our impressions of a landscape composition are visual. Take a look at your landscape and reduce the scene to its primary

elements. The primary element that we see is lines. The lines of tree trunks, the house, the edges of beds. Lines are the primary part of a landscape that appeals to the eye. Vertical lines are the most powerful. A cypress reaching skyward is a forceful landscape element that moves your eye upward. A cypress standing alone and with no other element to balance it can be a disturbing force in the landscape; it would be improved by a strong horizontal line, such as a hedge or wall, to give it balance. Curved lines are leisurely and restful, gentle movement from one degree of curve to the next. Jagged or crooked lines, on the other hand, are irritating. A free-flowing, easy-blending curve gives an effect of balance and completeness. Lines give the landscape balance and unity. If a garden design doesn't look right, your first thought should be to study its lines.

Simplicity should be your guiding principle in design. A common misconception is that design must include fountains, ponds or even statuary. These have their place but can be fussy and even pompous in the home garden. Simplicity and naturalness are far more satisfying than abundance of ornamentation. Another common mistake, particularly for the beginning gardener, is to become interested immediately in details. Don't get bogged down in interesting detail before you have the basics solved. Get your skeleton plan well defined and then move on to details such as the individual plants and garden ornamentation.

Putting It All Together

One way of looking at garden design is to think about creating garden "rooms." The best way to understand garden rooms is to compare them to rooms in your house. Each room is used for a different purpose: whether it be the private space of a bedroom or the family space of the living room or den. The same principle can be applied to your outside rooms, because they have different features for different purposes. The area around the terrace or swimming pool is used for recreation. The woodland path is made for strolling, with an inviting bench to encourage sitting. Different spaces must be well defined and should flow easily from one area to another just as the rooms in a house do. Be consistent in your design and keep the elements of your landscape scheme in good scale with each other.

Once you have decided on your garden rooms, where to put your border or how the front-walk flower bed will be arranged, you are ready to start placing your plants on your plan. Lay your garden areas out one at a time. It's a good idea to plan as much as you can in advance, but you need not complete all the rooms in one season. In fact, it's probably better not to do them all at once. Doing one at a time will be more manageable and give you more time to enjoy the fruits of your efforts. And that means it will be more likely that you will want to make the effort next time.

Start with your shrubs before going to perennials and annuals. Shrubs are the anchor plants. They can give balance, symmetry and form to the garden. If you are planting in front of the house and intend to use shrubs for foundation plantings, relate the vertical structure (or lines) to the horizontal plane of the landscape, the house and

surrounding trees. These will help you decide on your shrubs. Consider the ultimate size of the shrub before you place it and consider what will be planted around and in front of it. Do not use shrubs that will grow too large to remain in scale and proportion; otherwise you must be prepared to do regular pruning. Be sure to note the height to the windows and do not place shrubs where they will grow up to block the light into the window.

For your annuals, perennials and bulbs, plan your beds in three areas: front, middle and back. In the front belong the shortest plants, from 5 to 12 inches. The middle will have the 1- to 3-foot plants. The back of the bed will be for the 3- to 5-foot-tall varieties. Perennials usually have a short season of bloom, from two to three weeks. Some, like lilies and goldenstar, are longer. And others, like hosta and ferns, are grown mostly for their foliage. On the other hand, annuals bloom continuously all summer and can fill in nicely those gaps left by the fading perennials.

Seasonality, height and spacing of your plants are all important considerations for laying out your garden.

Color

Color is so important in designing your garden that entire books have been dedicated to nothing but this subject. Color is one of the elements in the design of a landscape that creates rhythm.

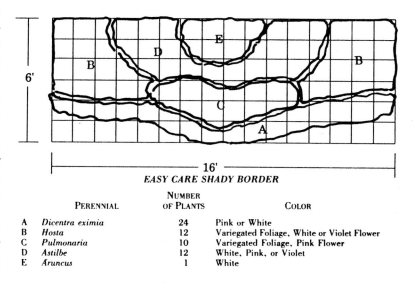

EASY CARE SHADY BORDER

	PERENNIAL	NUMBER OF PLANTS	COLOR
A	*Dicentra eximia*	24	Pink or White
B	*Hosta*	12	Variegated Foliage, White or Violet Flower
C	*Pulmonaria*	10	Variegated Foliage, Pink Flower
D	*Astilbe*	12	White, Pink, or Violet
E	*Aruncus*	1	White

Drifts of hostas and daylilies intermingle along a woodland path.

Rhythm is the recurrence of similar forms, lines, masses or color, or it may be a combination of these. Plan your colors well and you will have a pleasing and effective rhythm and design. Color is accent. Any portion of the landscape can be made to stand out more prominently by the addition of color. A shrub will be more dominant if covered with a mass of blooms. A wall or fence becomes more interesting if a flowering vine winds along it. Color can give fire and life to any area, including shade.

Limiting yourself to two or three colors is an easy way to plan a garden. A soft, romantic look is achieved with pastel pinks, blues and purples blended together in a harmonious way. Try the hot colors for a big, bold statement, using reds, oranges and yellow. When using color combinations keep in mind that the cool colors of blue and purple seem to recede and the warm colors of red and yellow give the illusion of moving forward. The receding of cool colors is particularly true for the shade where light may already be at a minimum. White and yellows are especially prominent in low-level light situations. Use these colors as companions to bring up the blues and purples. In shade, use lighter colors—mauve, peach and lavender—against the dark greens of shrubs.

The all-white garden, popularized by the great gardener Gertrude Jekyll, is a spectacular sight, often called a "moonlight" garden because the whites are enhanced by the absence of light at dusk and twilight. This is an excellent type of garden for shade. Make a moonlight garden

with fragrant plants near the sitting area in your garden and the experience will be one to remember. Another interesting and often overlooked color for the garden is green. There are multitudes of shades of green, ranging from the deep forest greens to the wonderful chartreuse and the soft, silvery greens. These are very important to the shade garden, where they will act to blend or knit colors and provide textures.

Textures and Patterns for Shady Design

Texture is usually given only slight consideration as an element of design. The garden that has been planned with consideration for textures and pattern will show a higher degree of style and finish. This is particularly true in shade gardening. There are many flowering plants for the shade, but some of the best plants for shade, especially deep shade, are foliage plants. These plants can create style and be a powerful architectural element.

HOSTAS: A WEALTH OF FOLIAGE FOR SHADY SPOTS

Hostas are exceptional plants and may be the most versatile and rewarding of all plants for the shade. Referred to by many as the "king of the shade," there is nothing so handsome nor so handy as the hosta. It is also called funkia or plantain lily.

Hosta is an old-fashioned plant that has seen a major resurgence in the last 15 years.

Its regained popularity is easy to understand. Hosta has few faults. It grows well in almost every part of the country and comes in a variety of colors, textures, sizes and shapes, and performs in every degree of shade. Hosta is ideally suited to our busy lifestyles—it is easy to grow, long lived and virtually carefree.

Hosta ranges in size from quite small to a spread of several feet. The leaves may be green, gold or blue, or variegated with yellow or white. Leaf texture may be smooth or puckered, shiny or matte. Hostas are usually grown for their foliage but all produce flowers of white, lavender or violet, some fragrant and very attractive to bees and hummingbirds. Although the leaves are deciduous, they can last as long as nine months in most areas. There are hundreds of species and cultivars from which to choose. Hosta is the ultimate easy-care plant for an informal woodland garden and a wide variety of other uses.

Using Hostas in the Garden

Hostas can be used in masses or as groundcovers. Combine them with your favorite plants or consider them on their own for a special or even a difficult area. Their handsome leaves can create bold patterns and rich textures.

EDGING: Used as an edging, hosta is delightful along garden paths and walkways. Small, gold hosta makes a particularly interesting edge. 'Gold Drop' and 'Gold Standard' are especially nice. Little hostas, such as *H. venusta*, looks charming planted around a small pool. *H. ventricosa* works well along the top of a rock wall or drooping over the edge and softening masonry construction. 'Ginko Craig' is a small edging plant that increases rapidly. 'Royal Standard', a larger hosta with fragrant blooms late in the season, can also be very effective along large ponds as well as for foundation plantings around your house.

DRIFTS: One of the best ways to create a natural effect with hosta is by planting it in drifts. A drift creates an effect similar to that of a groundcover, but the plants are spaced to look as

if they occurred naturally, usually more thickly planted in the center, thinning gradually into another variety of hosta or other plants. Drifts look particularly good trailing down a slope or in a curved bed in a small lot. Drifts work best with at least a dozen or so of the same plant. A collection of few plants of the same variety may appear uneven and will not give you that natural effect.

GROUNDCOVERS: If you have large shady areas to cover, hosta —unsurpassed as a groundcover—is your answer. Masses of the medium and large inexpensive cultivars grow quickly to fill a space and shade out weeds. Their spreading roots can check soil erosion on steep banks. *Hosta* 'August Moon' with gold leaves and 'Aurea Marginata' with gold edges are excellent groundcovers for dark, shady areas. 'Honeybells' and *H. lancifolia* are both old-fashioned favorites that also perform well in shade and in some sun. I have *H. lancifolia* under 100-year-old linden trees, and they have grown there for years. Every August they offer the most spectacular display of purple flowers in the deepest shade.

ACCENT PLANTS: Two or three plants of the larger hosta varieties, such as *H. Sieboldiana* 'Elegans', make a wonderfully bold accent in the garden. 'Elegans' is strikingly textured and has some of the bluest leaves. *H.* 'Frances Williams' is one of the most highly rated and sought-after hostas with blue-green leaves and a broad golden edge. 'Piedmont Gold' is an eye-

Foliage plants can create exciting textures and patterns:

Maidenhair fern, Lamium *and* hosta

Three varieties of Euonymus *combined with* Hosta

Liriope *with* Pulmonaria *'Mrs. Moon'*

catcher, and its yellow leaves persist throughout the season. A dramatic accent is *H. plantaginea*, sometimes called the August lily because of its large white flowers that bloom in late summer—also nicely fragrant.

Use a variety of hostas to create bold patterns and rich textures. Here is a handsome mixture of H. albomarginata, H. 'Francee', H. 'Frances Williams' and H. Sieboldiana 'Elegans'.

The striking differences in hosta leaf shape and color can be used to great effect in the shade garden.

Hosta 'Honeybells'

COMBINATIONS: By combining several different hostas with shade-loving companions such as *Liriope*, *Lamiastrum* and your favorite begonias, you can create visual symphonies with surprising ease. Try also *Astilbe*, columbine and bleeding heart. In full or dense shade, the delicate fronds of ferns blend beautifully with hosta. The largest hosta with the boldest foliage make an effective composition with high-shading trees or tree stumps. They also work well at the base of black alder, vine maple, birch or bald cypress in wet soil. I plant daffodil with hosta regularly because the daffodil blooms before the hosta emerges.

Recommended Hostas

'AUGUST MOON'. Large yellow leaves with white flowers.
'FRANCES WILLIAMS' (also sold as *H. Sieboldiana* 'Frances Williams' and *H. Sieboldiana* 'Aurea Marginata'). Blue-green leaves with yellow edges, pale lilac flowers. One of the finest hostas in cultivation. Ranks as the number one hosta according to the American Hosta Association.

'GINKO CRAIG'. A dwarf hybrid with blue flowers and light green leaves that are narrowly edged in white. A good edging plant that increases rapidly.
'GOLD STANDARD'. Light gold leaves edged with green, lavender flowers.
'HONEYBELL'. An older cultivar with light green leaves and fragrant, pale lavender flowers.
H. PLANTAGINEA (August lily). Pale green leaves with very fragrant, trumpet-shaped white flowers.
H. SIEBOLDIANA 'Elegans'. Bold bluish green leaves, white flowers. A very fine hosta.
H. UNDULATA 'Albomarginata'. White-edged green leaves, lavender flowers.
H. VENTRICOSA. Broad glossy green leaves, violet flowers. One of the finest hostas for both foliage and flowers.
H. VENUSTA. A dwarf variety with green leaves and lilac flowers. A good edging plant.
'PIEDMONT GOLD'. Ruffled and puckered leaves, white flowers. An excellent yellow variety best grown in partial shade.
'ROYAL STANDARD'. Yellow-green, puckered foliage, fragrant white flowers.

FERNS

To most gardeners the words *ferns* and *shade* are synonymous. These shade-loving plants are all too often overlooked because of their lack of blossoms. But they are perfect for the cool, shady places in your garden, for few plants impart such a light, airy and cooling effect on the landscape. The Victorians loved ferns and grew them extensively in their gardens and in their homes. Ferns were viewed as the most ornamental of foliage plants and for this reason they are enjoying a long overdue renaissance.

Ferns come in all shapes and

sizes with exquisite foliage that many describe as "architectural." And, indeed, large ferns in the back of the border can look very architectural. Ferns are ideal for the woodland garden and in the mixed border. Many are formal enough to be grown as foundation plantings. The Victorians grew them in containers, and you might try this along the patio or terrace.

Large Ferns

The best ferns for dramatic impact are the *Osmunda*. This is a strong, stately plant that grows to 5 feet or more in favorable conditions, 3 feet in drier conditions. All *Osmunda* are excellent for foundation plantings for they don't become overgrown as the years pass nor do they trap moisture that may rot wood along the foundation.

There are three species of *Osmunda*—the interrupted fern (*O. Claytoniana*), the cinnamon fern (*O. cinnamomea*) and the royal fern (*O. regalis*). The cinnamon fern may have the best autumn color, turning a beautiful yellow after frost. The ostrich fern (*Matteuccia pensylvanica*) provides a handsome 3-foot display all summer. Many consider it the most formal of the larger ferns. It makes a beautiful stand along the banks of a stream, where it is helpful for checking erosion. The large ferns are good if you have a wooded area near a formal garden and need plantings for a transitional area between the woods and the perennials. They can also hide the unsightly legginess of older rhododendron and azalea.

Medium Ferns

There is no limit to the selection of medium ferns. They combine well with woodland plants and with other ferns too. The best ferns for shady spots in this category are the genus *Dryopteris*, the shield ferns. Most reach 2 to 3 feet and are evergreen, making them nice year 'round.

The Christmas fern (*Polystichum acrostichoides*) is fully evergreen even in severe-winter areas. It's one of the best ferns for the northeast. It has very dark fronds often collected for holiday greenery. No shade garden should be without the native maidenhair fern (*Adiantum pedatum*). It is one of the loveliest of ferns, with delicate, light green, arching leaves. It prefers dense shade. Several people have told me they haven't had good luck with maidenhair fern and find it difficult to grow. The key is keeping maidenhair moist. The sensitivity fern (*Onoclea sinsibilis*) and the lady fern (*Athyrium Filix-femina*) are both readily available ferns that make very good plants for the shade garden and provide nice texture variations.

Any of the medium ferns can be used as a foliage background in the perennial garden or in lieu of the traditional yew or privet hedge.

The ostrich fern nestled among impatiens and elephant's ears gives a tropical feel to this garden.

BURPEE'S TIPS FOR HOSTAS

◆ *The amount of puckering on the leaves dictates usefulness under trees. Those heavily puckered catch rain drippings from the leaves, as well as seedpods, spent blossoms and the like. Glossy or smooth-leafed plants are less prone to tree droppings.*

◆ *Hostas will grow in deep shade if you plant them in an appropriately deep hole, cleaned of competitive roots, to reduce competition.*

◆ *As a rule of thumb, yellow-leafed and variegated forms need protection from direct sun, whereas blue forms require partial shade.*

◆ *Do not plant hosta in beds of ivy or pachysandra because it won't win the root competition.*

The Japanese painted fern is one of the most beautiful of all ferns.

FERN GUIDE

Name	Type	Height/ Spread	Shade Exposure	Soil	Remarks or Notes on Planting Care and Use
Adiantum pedatum (maidenhair fern)	Deciduous	18 inches/ 18 inches	All shade	Acid, moist	Very hardy with attractive texture; one of the loveliest ferns; spreads slowly
Asplenium bulbiferum (mother fern, mother spleenwort)	Evergreen	6 to 12 inches/ 12 inches	Full, deep	Neutral to slightly acid	Spreads slowly
Asplenium trichomanes (maidenhair spleenwort)	Evergreen	6 inches/ 8 to 12 inches	Medium, full	Neutral to acid	Good for rock crevices and mossy, north-facing walls
Athyrium Filix-femina (lady fern)	Deciduous	1½ feet/ 3 feet	Medium, full	Neutral, wet	Large, showy, lace-cut; tattered in late summer
Athyrium goeringianum 'Pictum' (Japanese painted fern)	Deciduous	12 inches/ 12 to 14 inches	Medium, full	Neutral, wet	Handsome and colorful
Blechnum (deer fern)	Evergreen	12 inches/ 18 inches	Full, deep	Acid, moist	Will grow in dark places better than any other fern
Dennstaedtia (hay-scented fern)	Deciduous	2 to 3 feet/ 3 feet	Light, medium, full	Neutral to acid	A notorious spreader; golden brown in autumn for long season of color
Dryopteris Filix-mas (male fern)	Evergreen	2 to 4 feet/ 4 feet	All shade	Neutral	Do not let dry out; Native American
Dryopteris Goldiana (Goldie's fern)	Evergreen	4 feet/ 4 feet	All shade	Neutral	Very large, impressive fern; usually the tallest fern in deep shade
Dryopteris intermedia (fancy fern)	Evergreen	2 feet/ 2 feet	Medium, full, deep	Neutral to acid	Handsome bluish green leaves

FERN GUIDE

NAME	TYPE	HEIGHT/ SPREAD	SHADE EXPOSURE	SOIL	REMARKS OR NOTES ON PLANTING CARE AND USE
Dryopteris marginalis (marginal shield fern)	Evergreen	2 to 3 feet/ 2½ feet	Medium, full, deep	Neutral	Easily established; withstands colder temperatures of northern areas
Matteuccia Struthiopteris (ostrich fern)	Deciduous	3 to 5 feet/ 4 to 8 feet	Light, medium, full	Neutral to acid, moist	Most formal of the larger ferns; good foundation plant; beautiful and architectural form; spreads by underground stolons
Nephrolepis (sword fern)	Evergreen	2 feet/ 2 feet	Light	Loose, acid	Tender fern will grow on tree trunks in tropical gardens
Onoclea sensibilis (sensitive fern)	Deciduous	2 to 3 feet/ 2 feet	Light, medium	Neutral to acid, wet	Needs moisture; spreads rapidly
Osmunda cinnamomea (cinnamon fern)	Deciduous	4 to 6 feet/ 2 to 3 feet	Light	Acid, wet	Very hardy; first fern of spring; white woolly fiddleheads
Osmunda regalis (royal fern)	Deciduous	4 to 6 feet/ 4 to 8 feet	Light, medium	Neutral to acid, wet	Golden spores resemble blooms
Polypodium virginianum (polypody fern)	Evergreen	6 to 8 inches/ 12 inches	Light, medium	Neutral	Grows well on rocks; vigorous and mat forming
Polystichum acrostichoides (Christmas fern)	Evergreen	3 feet/ 5 feet	Medium, full, deep	Neutral	Best fern for the Northeast; good for erosion; often collected for greenery at Christmas
Polystichum munitum (sword fern)	Evergreen	3 feet/ 3 to 4 feet	Medium, full, deep	Acid	Grows particularly well in West and Northwest; very handsome plant

GROUNDCOVERS FOR SHADE

Groundcovers may be the perfect answer for a number of those difficult shaded areas. They can carpet bare earth, substitute for grass, bind sandy soils, underplant trees and shrubs and check erosion on hillsides. Many can live where nothing else will grow, with little or no maintenance. One of the main reasons I like to use them is that most of them survive neglect.

Groundcovers are tough and durable, low-growing and rapid-spreading plants. They are usually perennials or shrubs, but a groundcover can be any plant that in fact will cover the ground. Its growth may be by means of underground runners, above-ground stolons, or clumps. Grass is the most widely used groundcover but it is not suitable for shade. The best plants for groundcovers are those with evergreen leaves that look nice the entire year. Pachysandra, myrtle (*Vinca minor*) and some of the ivies are among the most

popular; sometimes they are referred to as "the unholy three" as they seem to be ubiquitous. Still, these plants are incorrigible workhorses as few others can boast.

The most common and certainly the most popular is pachysandra, also known as Japanese spurge. You cannot drive through many neighborhoods without seeing at least half a dozen different uses for this groundcover. It is tough, hardy and durable, and is excellent under large shade trees, open areas and under shrubs. One note of caution: Pachysandra should not be planted directly under broad-leafed evergreens as it removes moisture and food from the soil.

Another excellent, and also very popular, groundcover is *Vinca minor*. Also known as common myrtle and periwinkle, this groundcover is sometimes considered the best because of its evergreen leaves, long life and lovely blue or white flowers. A particularly interesting variety is *V. minor* 'Variegata', which produces yellow variegated leaves and pale blue flowers. This variety is one you don't see very often, but can be very effective in a shady area. Plant your spring bulbs with this groundcover. It also trails nicely over walls.

Rounding out the trio is the *Hedera* genus, ivies. Ivy is evergreen, spreads rapidly, checks erosion, climbs or covers and requires little maintenance. English ivy (*Hedera helix*) is the most popular kind of ivy with more than 200 different varieties grown in North America. It

prospers in dense shade and even in poor soil. One of the hardiest varieties is *H. helix* 'Baltica' and few others can equal it in its groundcovering ability. In addition to use as groundcovers, ivies are handy for covering walls and fences. Contrary to popular belief, ivy is *not* good for a living tree, so keep your ivy restrained at the bottom of the tree on the bark. As a general rule, ivies with green leaves are very shade tolerant. Those with variegated or yellow leaves prefer more light and are usually less hardy.

Other groundcovers that can be very interesting are bugleweed (*Ajuga reptans*) and barrenwort (*Epimedium*). Some *Ajuga* are a purple bronze in partial shade and add a delightful colorful contrast to rhododendron, azalea and fern. *Epimedium* is a clump maker, grown for its elegant foliage and small flowers. It is easy to grow, is hardy and has been known to survive under maples where pachysandra and myrtle have failed. Their spring flowers are particularly lovely. A personal favorite of mine is dead nettle (*Lamium maculatum*). The 'Beacon Silver' variety has unusual silver leaves with narrow green edges and pink flowers. This colorful groundcover will brighten any shady area except the very darkest.

For a grasslike groundcover that never needs mowing, try lilyturf (*Liriope*): evergreen, arching tufts of green, grasslike foliage with large lilac flowers that bloom in late summer. (In cold climates the leaves may turn

Epimedium makes a perfect groundcover for those difficult, dark areas under trees.

yellow and should be removed before new growth begins.) This is a reliably hardy plant everywhere but may burn back where winter freezing is most severe. Lilyturf makes an excellent edging plant and is especially appropriate for the spare look that characterizes Oriental-style gardens. For partially shaded, moist sites leadwort (*Plumbago*) has brilliant blue flowers in late summer or fall and leaves that take on a reddish hue in fall. Another plant responding well to moist shade is the herb sweet woodruff (*Galium odoratum*), which makes a fine companion for forget-me-nots or with shrubs and spring bulbs. Trailing wintercreeper (*Euonymus*) offers a range of sizes, color and textures depending on the variety. One of the smallest and best suited to limited spaces is *E. Fortunei*. For steep, rocky banks consider Hall's honeysuckle (*Lonicera japonica* 'Halliana'). This has traditionally been a favorite for porches but it is excellent for preventing erosion. One word of caution, however; this particular variety is aggressive and can become a weedy, shrubby vine in the southern United States.

PERENNIALS FOR GROUNDCOVERS

Any plant can be used as a groundcover if there is enough of it, but a number of perennials are especially to be recommended as groundcovers for the shade. Plantain lily (*Hosta*) certainly tops almost everyone's list as the most versatile plant for shade and we offer a considerable amount of information dedicated exclusively to this workhorse of the shade garden earlier in this chapter. What makes hosta so valuable as a groundcover is that it is very hardy, exceptionally long lived and comes in an inspiring variety of shapes and shades of green.

Ideal as a groundcover, along a path or in the front of the border, bergenia has evergreen foliage with lovely lavender-pink flowers that appear in midspring. It grows quickly and easily and is tolerant of most soils. One of the finest characteristics of bergenia is that its foliage takes on a burnished hue in fall and winter, giving this plant year-'round beauty.

The spotted leaves of lungwort (*Pulmonaria*) provide the perfect carpet for a shady corner. This is a hardy groundcover that grows 15 inches tall, has delightful spring flowers and interesting, spotted leaves. *P. saccharata* 'Mrs. Moon' is an especially handsome variety with heavily marbled foliage that produces an overall silvery or white effect. *P. augustifolia* (also called *P. azurea*) is atypical, having plain, dark green leaves. The clusters of pink buds open to a rich blue, making this an ideal underplanting for forsythia. There is also a white form called *P. vulgaris* 'Alba' and a very good dwarf form 'Salmon Glow' with early blooms.

THE SHADE PLANTING AND GROWING GUIDE

SOIL

All gardeners learn the hard way about soil: by poor or odd growth or even the expiration of plants. Virtually everything the plant needs to live comes from the soil, and creating good soil is the most important thing you can do for plants. Soil is their lifeline, and by starting from the ground up you will have healthy, bigger and better plants. All gardeners end up with the same conclusion: It always comes down to good soil.

If you're a first-time gardener or are preparing a new bed in your garden, you must determine what kind of soil you have. Soil is the surface area of the earth that supports plant life. It is made up of inorganic minerals, air, water and organic matter. The topsoil, or upper layer, is usually darker; it contains organic matter known as humus. It is in the topsoil that your plants will develop the roots that supply them with most of their nutrients. The subsoil beneath the topsoil is usually more dense and harder to dig. Both soil levels can and should be improved for the health of your plants.

Most soils consist of a mixture of sand, clay and silt. The ideal sowing soil, loam, balances all three of these. What sort of soil you have depends on the proportion of these three elements. An analysis of your soil will determine the exact composition, but you can make a rough judgment by taking a handful of the soil and squeezing it in your hand.

Sandy soil feels gritty and doesn't hold together well. It is easy to work with, drains well and is usually rich in oxygen. Because it drains so well, it dries out quickly. Fertilizer added to sandy soil leaches quickly away. Water and nutrients must be replaced often. Sandy soils are often referred to as "light" soils.

Silt consists of particles smaller than sand and holds together better when squeezed. It has fewer air spaces than sand and thus drainage is slower.

Clay is often referred to as "heavy" soil. When you squeeze clay it forms a solid ball. There is little space among the particles for air and water to circulate, and drainage is quite poor. Clay holds more nutrients, but they are unavailable to plants until the clay is improved with the addition of organic matter. Plants often get waterlogged and rot. This dense soil is hard for a plant's roots to penetrate. It is difficult to get plants started in this soil, but once they are established most do well.

Loam is the ideal, well-balanced soil. It holds together well when squeezed and breaks up when you tap it. It is often referred to as "friable" soil because it breaks up easily, holds moisture well and encourages organic activity. Earthworms find this soil inviting.

This rough test will give you an idea of what you'll be working with, but it's wise to have your soil tested. A soil test is inexpensive. The

The big, bold leaves of Hosta 'Frances Williams' *make this a superb accent plant.*

Clay soil

Sandy soil

Loamy soil

easiest method is to take or send a sample of your soil to your local agricultural extension unit (usually listed in the telephone book). Another method is to purchase a soil testing kit and do it yourself. The soil test will tell you what the deficiencies of the soil are, and this will help you determine what you need to add to improve it.

The soil test will also tell you the pH of your soil. The pH scale is the measurement of acidity and alkalinity expressed as a number from 0 to 14, with the least number being pure acid and the greatest number being pure lye; 7.0 is the neutral point, neither acid nor alkaline. Slightly acid soil of pH 6.5 is what we aim for, good for most plants. There are exceptions to this and many of those happen to be shade plants—rhododendron and hydrangea are two examples that require a more acidic soil. Other plants need a bit more alkaline to survive. Few plants will survive in soil more acid than pH 4 or more alkaline than pH 8.

Improving Your Soil

Add the necessary materials to improve your soil. To reduce acidity of the soil, use finely ground limestone. Dig the soil 8 to 10 inches deep in fall. Spread lime evenly over the surface and rake in. The application rate is 50 pounds per 1,000 square feet to raise it one pH point. To increase the acidity of the soil use flowers of sulfur, available at most garden centers. Every soil will benefit by the addition of organic matter. Organic matter is the natural way of improving your soil, and adding organic matter should be done every year to replace the nutrients used. Your soil is steadily depleted by needy plants and needs replenishment in order to be able to support them.

The ideal soil for the shade garden is a mildly acid soil, rich with organic matter, light with some sand, and containing only a small amount of clay. As most shade plants are woodland plants by nature, we need to recreate the woodland or forest floor to make them at home. This means that two-thirds of your soil should be rich humus or organic matter. Compost, leaf mold, peat moss and manure are all excellent sources of organic matter.

Manures of farm animals are probably the most commonly used organic matter for improving the soil. They are high in nitrogen and other nutrients and improve the tilth of the soil. Manure from cows, horses and mules are best (and can be purchased dehydrated and well rotted in bags); chicken and rabbit manures can be used only when very well rotted, as they are otherwise caustic and will harm your plants. All manures should be well rotted when applied so the plants are not burned by the ammonia given off during decomposition. Well-rotted manure looks like dark, rich soil and doesn't have an odor. It is available commercially in bags, but you can check a local farm—they are usually glad for someone just to cart it away. Again, fresh stable manure should never be used, with one exception, and that is when you have created a new bed with no plants. Fresh manure can be applied in the fall; over the following four to five months, with occasional turning, it should be decomposed by spring.

Peat moss is another good soil conditioner. Peat, or peat moss, is made up of deposits of plant matter that has decomposed in water or a boggy area. Its value is its ability to absorb and hold moisture. It lightens the soil and is extremely useful for maintaining cool, moist conditions in wild or woodland gardens and around shrubs. It doesn't have a lot of plant-food content, so it's a good idea to use it with well-rotted manure when additional nutrients are wanted.

COMPOSTING

One of the best ways to add organic matter to your soil is by adding compost. Compost is simply a means of returning organic material otherwise discarded back to the soil in the form of humus. It's simple, inexpensive and environmentally sound. Materials for compost making include kitchen scraps, leaves, grass clippings and garden debris. All this is probably material you are now hauling to the curb for municipal disposal. Mounting solid waste disposal problems and awareness of the environment have encouraged Congress as well as individuals to rethink how we view our trash. By starting a compost pile you will discover a handy way to deal with your garbage and get an excellent soil conditioner for your garden.

Compost is made by layering vegetable matter and organic material between thin layers of garden soil. Keep the pile moist—not wet—so it can decompose. Your pile will reduce garbage such as kitchen wastes (including coffee grounds and tea leaves), sawdust and even dirt from your vacuum cleaner into usable humus in a matter of months.

The rotting or decomposition happens from inside the compost pile where temperatures can reach as high as 160° to 170°F. Decay will happen quicker if you turn the pile with a pitchfork every week or two. Soil is added to introduce microorganisms and worms that will encourage the breakdown of the compost material. Add a thin layer of lime and an occasional layer of wood ashes, particularly if you have a lot of leaves in your compost. The lime is to offset the acidity of the leaves and the wood ashes add phosphorus and potash.

Organic matter in the compost pile includes microorganisms (bacteria) and macroorganisms (earthworms, nematodes and insects). As long as oxygen is present, fast-acting aerobic bacteria readily decompose material, breaking it down into beneficial plant food. By turning the compost pile often you reactivate the oxygen-consuming organisms and speed things up. When oxygen is used up, composting continues, but more slowly, because it's being accomplished by anaerobic bacteria alone. Winter months when the temperatures can reach freezing will also slow the process.

Starting a compost pile can be as easy as making a pile of leaves behind the garage, but it's a lot easier if you enclose your pile to contain it and make it easier to handle. There are many different types of compost container on the market, some compact enough to sit right outside the kitchen door. You can also make your own with a few posts and some chicken wire. We made our own, finding the commercial ones too small.

You can make a compost bin out of almost anything—just be sure to leave room for the air circulation so vital to the bacteria that break down the vegetable matter. If you use a large drum or barrel, punch holes in the side. One side of the container should be removable for easy access to the compost. Your compost is ready to use when it turns black or dark brown and has disintegrated into small pieces. This is when it is ready to be distributed to your borders, woodland paths, around trees and shrubs. Add compost to your soil as least once a year to replenish the nutrients your plants need to stay healthy.

What to put in the compost pile—	What not to put in the compost pile:
remember that the smaller the pieces are, the faster they will decompose:	*Meat, grease, oil and bones, because they will attract rats and other vermin*
Leaves (except black walnut)	*Coal and charcoal ashes, because they contain toxic residues*
Grass clippings (untreated)	*Weeds with seedpods*
Fruits and vegetables	*Diseased plants*
Nonanimal kitchen scraps (corn husks, carrot tops, etc.)	*Grass clippings or any other plant material that has been chemically treated*
Tea leaves	*Any plastic materials*
Coffee grounds	*Colored newspapers and magazines*
Eggshells	*Manure from dogs, cats or humans, because it can transmit disease*
Farm animal manure	
Twigs	
Wood ashes	
Seaweed (wash off salt)	
Sawdust and lumber shavings	
Garden debris (tops of perennials cut back in the fall, deadheaded flowers, etc.)	
Silt removed from the bottoms of ponds	

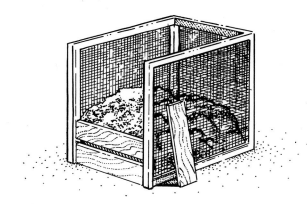

This compost starter bin is easy to make from four 4-foot posts, set in a square rectangle, wrapped in chicken wire. If the chicken wire is secured loosely on the fourth side, the bin can be opened easily for removal of compost or for working the compost pile.

FERTILIZERS

There are 16 elements known to be necessary for healthy plant growth. Most of these are trace elements that we don't need to worry about replenishing. Nitrogen, phosphorus and potassium are the elements needed in the largest amounts; they are used up the fastest, therefore they should be replaced regularly. Whatever nutrients you need to add to your soil depends on those nutrients already present and on the soil pH and texture. The best fertilizer recommendations can come only from a soil test.

Nitrogen promotes good leaf and stem growth and is responsible for plants' good green color. Excess nitrogen will produce too much leaf and stem growth instead of producing a good root system or even flowers. Phosphorus is essential for root development and is vital to photosynthesis. It also plays a key role in the production of flowers. Always try to use some extra phosphorus when transplanting as this will help promote the root growth. Last, potassium promotes strong plant growth, important for hardiness and disease resistance. If you regularly add organic matter to your soil, you will probably not need to add any inorganic or "chemical" fertilizers. At Burpee, we feel it is always best to use the organic methods first and turn to inorganic only when necessary. In addition to organic fertilizers from animal and plant waste, there are bone meal, blood meal and cottonseed meal. All organic fertilizers are slow acting and nonburning.

Manure is the best source of naturally occurring nitrogen and is particularly useful if you have added a lot of peat to your soil, as peat doesn't have much in the way of plant nutrients. Liquid fish emulsion diluted according to the manufacturers' directions is also a good source of nitrogen.

The best source of organic phosphorus is bone meal. You can also use horn meal, but it is not as easy to find. Bone meal should be used with manure because manure is comparatively low in phosphorus.

Wood ashes are your best source of organic potassium. Be sure to save those ashes from your fireplace or woodburning stove all winter. (Or ask a neighbor to save them for you.) If you have a lot of leaves in your compost pile, wood ashes are also a good source of potassium.

Commercial fertilizer ingredients are explained by the numbers printed on their containers, 5-10-5 or 10-6-4, for example. The three numbers represent percentages of nitrogen, phosphorus and potassium, in that order; this is called the "NPK rating." All-purpose fertilizers are usually made from inorganic chemical compounds such as ammonium sulfate (for nitrogen), superphosphate (for phosphorus), and sulfate of potash (for potassium). Commercial fertilizers come in granular forms that break down quickly and in slow-release formulas that break down slowly and stay in the soil longer. The slow-release formulas are usually used for trees and shrubs.

WORKING THE SOIL

Most shade plants will do very nicely in a 2-1-1 soil blend of humus, sand and loam. It is highly unlikely that you will be lucky enough to have this soil just waiting for you on your property, so you will have to prepare your new bed by making improvements to your existing soil. For a new bed, this means double-digging the soil. Many people avoid double-digging, thinking it too difficult and that it is unnecessary to dig down more than 4 to 6 inches. This is perfectly fine for such shallow-rooted plants as annuals, but many perennials and shrubs are deep-rooted and will benefit greatly by improving the soil 18 to 24 inches down. Here the importance of deep penetration of the soil cannot be overemphasized, for these plants are going to be around for some time, and a good beginning is well worth the effort.

Double-digging requires that you remove the topsoil and the.

subsoil from your bed 18 to 24 inches deep. You can temporarily put the unearthed soil either at the other end of the bed or place it on a tarp next to the bed. (I use a tarp because I tend to add so much organic matter that all of the original soil doesn't get returned to the bed. Excess soil is taken to the compost pile.) Add humus or organic matter to the bottom of the hole. Then mix more humus with the displaced soil to make loam, work in half as much sand, and fill in the hole. Do this in approximately 2- to 3-foot strips. The process continues strip by strip until you reach the end of your plot. It seems like a great deal of work, but it is worth it. If you are preparing a large area, rent a Rototiller. Run it back and forth over an area and it will break up the soil to about a depth of 8 inches. Because Rototillers do not go deeper than this you will have to remove the first layer and rototill the next layer.

WATERING

Watering seems like the easiest of tasks, yet it is probably done more inaccurately than any other gardening chore. It is a basic function of the planting process and, unfortunately, many plants are lost due to improper watering methods.

WHEN TO WATER: The time to water is largely determined by the type of soil. If you have improved your soil and created a balanced, loamy soil, once every week to 10 days should be sufficient for established plants. If you are unsure when to water, just dig down to see if the soil is moist under the surface, or pick up a handful of soil and squeeze it into a ball: If it crumbles when you try to shape it, water is necessary. Sandy soils drain faster and watering may need to be done more frequently. Clay soils retain moisture better and probably need to be watered every 10 to 14 days (depending on weather). Most plants need about 1 inch of water every week; use a rain gauge to help determine whether water is needed.

Newly placed plants need to be kept moist, as do seedlings and newly planted trees or shrubs, because roots need water to become established. Water more frequently during dry spells. Plants grown against walls or hedges may need watering even after a rainfall due to the angle of the falling rain. Plants high on a slope will dry out faster than those growing at the bottom of the hill.

HOW TO WATER: The way that you water is important. Try not to wet the leaves. Overhead watering can create an environment for insects or disease. It is best to water in the morning and at ground level. Don't water in the evening because disease organisms can get a headstart on wet foliage at night, when leaves don't have the sun's rays to dry them.

WATER DEEPLY: When watering, be sure to soak the soil to at least a foot deep. Watering less than this will encourage shallow rooting, where roots can be burned by the hot sun. Use a soaker hose or a drip irrigation system if you have them. If you don't, you can use the old-fashioned trick of sinking an old coffee can with holes punched in it at intervals among the plants. Fill them with water and they will soak the ground.

CONSERVE WATER: Water is becoming scarce and is more than ever a precious resource. Use a drip system hose, or get a timer for your sprinkler system, and never let water run out into the curb or down a slope wastefully. To prevent sacrificing moisture to evaporation, avoid watering on a windy day. Prevent moisture loss by mulching. Conserve water by using it correctly.

MULCHING

Mulching is a garden practice that will benefit your plants greatly. A mulch is any substance used to cover the ground around your garden plants. Mulching is an ancient practice and an adaptation of the natural process in much the same way that nature provides a protective covering of leaves in the woods.

ADVANTAGES OF MULCHING

CONSERVES MOISTURE: The greatest advantage to mulching is conservation of moisture in the soil. It keeps moisture from evaporating from the soil surface. In drier climates or during prolonged hot weather this is particularly helpful in protecting the soil from the direct rays of the sun and drying wind. Mulch also absorbs rain and keeps the moisture locked in.

CONTROLS WEEDS: Mulch greatly reduces the amount of weeding required. This is especially true of annual weeds. Weed carefully before applying

Mulch not only conserves moisture and controls weeds, but can also line paths effectively.

a mulch and this covering will prevent weed seed from establishing. Be assured, however, that some weeds will find their way in, but weeding will be reduced substantially with a layer of mulch.

UNIFORM SOIL TEMPERATURES: A layer of mulch will keep the soil cooler in summer and warmer in winter. Uniform soil temperatures will benefit the bacteria in your soil by keeping down high summer temperatures they find harmful. It provides cooler temperatures for those plants such as clematis that perform best when their roots are cooler. In winter, it keeps the soil several degrees warmer, protecting less hardy plants from frost penetration. In addition, mulch serves as insulation to prevent injury to root stocks. Keeping soil cooler will also attract earthworms closer to the top of the soil. When the soil is too warm they retreat to the cooler subsoil.

IMPROVES SOIL STRUCTURE AND TILTH: Many mulches are organic, and as organic matter breaks down it works its way into the topsoil, where it improves the soil structure and tilth (soil condition). This increases water penetration and provides better aeration for the growth of roots. Decomposing organic mulch adds nutrients to the soil, thereby improving soil fertility.

PREVENTS SOIL EROSION: A layer of mulch will prevent rain

from washing soil away. This is true even for slopes and hills.

DISADVANTAGES OF MULCH

There are a few disadvantages to mulching, but they are minor compared to the benefits mulching provides.

ATTRACTS PESTS: The biggest problem is that of attracting pests. Slugs can hide in mulch. A sprinkling of wood ashes or a commercial slug collar placed around the bottom of the plant will help keep them in check.

Mice and other rodents often root around in mulch looking for food and can be destructive to plants. Trapping is the safest way to rid yourself of these critters. Do not use poison if you enjoy the birds, as robins will often root around in mulch for the occasional worm.

PLANT ROT: Many plants are sensitive to moisture over the winter and when too much water builds up around the base of the plant, this causes rotting and the plant dies. This is particularly true of foxglove, coralbell and blanketflower. Mulch around these plants, but leave the space around the base bare.

DO NOT MULCH YOUNG PLANTS: Young plants should not be mulched until they are large enough not to be smothered by the mulch. Make sure they are well established. Never mulch newly seeded areas or young seedlings, for the same reason.

MULCHING MATERIALS

SHREDDED LEAVES: Autumn leaves are available almost everywhere and are excellent for shrubs and perennials. The leaves should be shredded because whole leaves can tamp down into an impenetrable mat. This can be easily done by running a lawn mower back and forth over a low pile of leaves. Place shredded leaves directly on the flower beds. Oak leaves mat down less than others such as maples and are especially recommended for rhododendron and azalea.

PINE NEEDLES: Pine needles are not only good mulching material, they are attractive, particularly in the shade garden, where plants tend to fill in less and bare soil can be an eyesore. They can simply be raked from under evergreens and spread around your plants. You can also use evergreen branches, which make good winter mulch for perennials. (This makes good use of discarded Christmas trees.)

WOOD CHIPS: Wood chips are readily available commercially and have become one of the home gardener's favorites. Wood chips are shredded bark, and the smaller the pieces, the faster they decompose and need to be replaced. Large wood chips should not be used with smaller plants; use them under shrubs. Wood shavings are not as practical as wood chips as they tend to blow away easily. Sawdust works well and it breaks down quickly, but it must be replaced several times over a season. Sawdust is excellent for rhododendron and azalea.

BUCKWHEAT HULLS: These look especially elegant in flower beds, but can be expensive if you need to cover a large area. They are tidy and lightweight, which is also their drawback— they tend to blow around rather easily.

COCOA SHELLS: This effective, lightweight mulch sold commercially has an attractive dark color that can set off lighter colors in your garden nicely. The chocolate aroma it gives off during the first couple of weeks is delightful, even if it seems somewhat odd.

STONE CHIPS OR GRAVEL: Used frequently around rock gardens or for an Oriental look, this makes for durable mulch that weeds can't usually penetrate. The drawback is you will need to add plant nutrients and humus. Soil compaction can damage roots. Stone chips and gravel are used more for paths.

BLACK PLASTIC: This is usually used with an additional, more attractive mulch to keep it in place and look neater. Black plastic will keep weeds down. Be sure to poke holes in it so rain can get through.

Perennials and annuals should be mulched once they are established in the spring. Fall-planted bulbs can be mulched any time after they are planted, but before freezing. Shrubs can be mulched at any time.

PLANT PORTRAITS

The plants discussed in this chapter offer great variety for shade gardening, and were selected for their popularity, easy culture and availability. Every plant is listed under its botanical (Latin) name and cross-referenced by its common name. Having the plant information you need listed under the scientifically correct name avoids confusion and misunderstanding. In the system of botanical nomenclature, every plant has a first name, the genus (indicated by the first Latin word), a grouping of plants with similar characteristics. Every plant has a second name, the species (the second Latin word), which further identifies qualities that plant shares with related plants. Because different plants may be known by the same common name, using botanical names is the one way to be sure of having the correct cultural information.

PLANT PORTRAIT KEY

Here is a guide to the symbols and terms we use throughout this section.

Latin name of the plant is in boldface italic.

Phonetic pronunciation of the Latin name is in parentheses.

Common name of the plant is in boldface type.

Symbols for:

◊ Fine for dry shade

✳ Cool-weather plant

❚ Long-lasting cut flower

❀ Long bloomer—6 weeks or longer

❀ Fragrant blooms or foliage

Grade of Difficulty: Plants that take the least amount of care are identified as "easy."

These plants are a good choice for beginning gardeners with little time.

Native American are the plants that were growing on the American continent when it was first colonized by Europeans. Many plants that are native to America are also native to other countries around the world.

Heights are for normal growth, but plants with very fertile soil and a longer growing season could grow taller. Conversely, with poor growing conditions, the plant could be shorter.

Zones: Check "The USDA Plant Hardiness Map of the United States" (page 94), based on average temperatures for each area—or zone—of the United States to see what zone you live in. For plants that are annuals, no zone designation is given, as the plant will manage practically anywhere; the length of time it will thrive during its single growing season will vary.

Viburnum plicatum 'Mariesii'

Acanthus spinosus

Aconitum napellus

Aaron's-beard; see *Hypericum*

Acanthus (ah-KANTH-us) **bear's-breech,** light to medium shade, easy, perennial. ⬥
Zones: 8 to 10 (6 and 7 with protection)
Height: 3 to 4 feet, dwarf 18 inches
Colors: Creamy white, rose, lavender
Characteristics: A statuesque plant, *Acanthus* is famous for the shape and simple beauty of its foliage. Its lustrous, deeply divided, green, hairy leaves can reach 3 feet in height. Blooming from late spring through early summer, *Acanthus* produces long spires of tubular flowers. Its unusual look and fountainlike shape makes it a good choice for massing as a stately accent plant or in the back of the border. It is evergreen and drought tolerant, and is seen much most frequently on the West Coast and in the Gulf States.

A. mollis is the most common species and the one from which Greek Corinthian columns took their inspiration. Its purple blooms flower in late spring. *A. mollis* 'Latifolius' has mauve flowers and is more heat tolerant, a better plant for southern climates. *A. spinosus* is also interesting but its thorny leaf margins make it difficult to work with; it features rose flowers and rigid, leathery leaves.
Cultural Information: Plant 3 to 4 feet apart in moist, rich soil with good drainage. It will do reasonably well in full sun in cooler climates. Plant in a warm, protected area and mulch

over winter in northern limits of its range. In California coastal regions the roots spread underground rapidly if not confined. Remove spent flower stalks. Watch for snails and slugs. Divide as necessary from October to March, but it is usually not needed.
Uses: Accent plant, in a border.
Recommended Varieties: Acanthus mollis, A. mollis 'Latifolius', *A. spinosus*.

Aconitum (ak-o-NY-tum) **monkshood,** light to medium shade, moderate, perennial. 🌡 ✳
Zones: 3 to 8
Height: 3 to 5 feet
Colors: Blue, white, pink, yellow or bicolor
Characteristics: Wonderful for late-summer, early-fall bloom when there are very few blue flowers available. *Aconitum* resembles its close relative the *Delphinium* but is much more reliable. These showy, hooded or helmet-shaped flowers grow on upright spikes. Their dark green foliage is divided with fingerlike leaves and is an asset in the garden all summer. The *A. Napellus* varieties bloom first, in late July. *A. Napellus* 'Bicolor' shows up in light shade with its white flowers edged with China blue. *A. Carmichaelii* has the darkest Wedgewood blue flowers in August and September. For yellow or creamy white flowers in July, grow *A. Vulparia*.
Cultural Information: Rich, moist soil is needed for growth, and afternoon shade and cooler climates are preferred; it performs poorly in hot and dry climates. Monkshood can be left undivided for many years. Divide

in the fall after it has finished flowering. It is not easily propagated from seed, sometimes taking 18 months to germinate and 3 years to flower. Plant in fall or spring with either tuberous roots or started plants. Established clumps resent transplanting. Mulch in May around each plant to help hold the moisture and cool the roots. **Caution:** All parts of this plant are poisonous if eaten and sap is extremely toxic—be careful when handling or cutting.
Uses: Back of a border, woodland walk, shady corners.
Recommended Varieties: Aconitum Napellus 'Bicolor', *A. Carmichaelii, A. Vulparia*.

Ajuga (ah-JOO-hah) **bugleweed,** light to medium shade, moderately easy, perennial.
Zones: 3 to 9
Height: 6 to 12 inches
Colors: Blue, blue-purple, creamy white, pink
Characteristics: An outstanding groundcover with bright blue flowers that appear from spring to early summer, usually May and June, on spikes 4 to 6 inches above the foliage. The leaves are 3 to 5 inches long, oval, and form in rosettes. *Ajuga* spreads easily and rapidly forms dense mats that are useful as a groundcover under dense trees.

A. reptans is the common bugleweed and readily available. With purple flowers and dark green foliage, this is a great creeper for quickly covering those bare spots. *A. reptans* 'Burgundy Glow' has beautifully variegated leaves of white, pink and rich purple. *A. reptans* 'Gaiety' has waxy, unusual leaves

of deep bronze. If you want an *Ajuga* that doesn't spread very rapidly, try *A. pyramidalis*. Its purple-bronze leaves and blue flowers look wonderful under rhododendron and other shrubs. *Cultural Information:* Plant 6 to 12 inches apart in moist, rich, well-drained soil with good air circulation in spring or fall. To propagate, cut off and re-plant new growth that springs from ends of runners. This plant should be contained, so don't plant next to a formal bed or edging a lawn. In the South, crown rot can be a problem, but it usually is not bothered by pests.
Uses: Path border, edging, groundcover.
Recommended Varieties: Ajuga reptans, A. pyramidalis, A. reptans 'Burgundy Glow', *A. reptans* 'Gaiety'.

Alchemilla (al-ke-MIL-ah) **lady's-mantle,** medium shade, easy, perennial. 🌡
Zones: 3 to 9
Height: 12 to 18 inches
Colors: Yellow, greenish yellow
Characteristics: This unusual-looking perennial produces frothy sprays of little flowers with a mound of yellow-green, rounded leaves. The flowers are an intense greenish yellow (now fashionably called chartreuse) that stand above the leaves in June through August. The flowers are perfect for arrangements as they last up to two weeks in water.

The most common lady's-mantle is *A. mollis* (*A. vulgaris* is very similar) and is considered by many to be a garden problem due to its rampant

spreading. It does spread rapidly but this can be controlled by removing the seed heads prior to maturity. The seedlings are easy to pull out and transplant. This is a good plant for problem areas. It makes a splendid groundcover that's quite showy. Use it to cascade down a shady slope. Its root system is thick, impenetrable to weeds, and will help check erosion. *A. mollis* is unequaled as a controller of excess space. Use it along a path, along a walkway or as a good informal edging. For a more well-behaved plant that does not spread as easily, use *A. × splendens*. Each of its leaves has a tiny white trimming and smaller chartreuse flowers.
Cultural Information: Plant lady's-mantle in any cool, moist soil except boggy soil. It blooms longer in cooler areas. To keep plants from free seeding, cut it back hard when the flowers have turned a darker yellow, usually in August. A new, neat clump of young leaves will grow again before the fall. Without this August trimming the plant can become invasive.
Uses: Groundcover, path border, drying.
Recommended: Alchemilla mollis, A. × splendens.

Algerian ivy; see *Hedera*

Alyssum, sweet; see *Lobularia*

Andromeda; see *Pieris*

Right: Ajuga *'Gaiety'*

Below left: Alchemilla mollis

Below right: Anemone × hybrida *'Alba'*

Anemone × hybrida (an-EM-on-e HI-brid-a) **Japanese anemone, hybrid anemone,** medium shade, easy, perennial. 🌡
Zones: 5 to 8
Height: 2 to 3½ feet
Colors: White, warm rose, pink
Characteristics: One of the most beautiful late-summer- and fall-blooming perennials, bridging the gap between the flowers of summer and late fall blooms. These single or double, long-stemmed flowers belong to the buttercup family and have no true petals but rather showy, petal-like sepals. The plant produces a moundlike habit with

Anemone × hybrida *'Queen Charlotte'*

branched stems. Excellent when grown in masses or naturalized in open spaces with deciduous trees. It has a wildflower character and works well in the woodland path or against shady walls or fences. *Anemone japonica* 'Honorine Jobert' is one of the prettiest and most popular white varieties; 'Margaréte' has semidouble, deep pink flowers; 'Queen Charlotte' has pink, semidouble flowers; 'September Charm' has single dark rose flowers with a lighter rose color on the inside for a striking shading effect.

Cultural Information: Cool, humus soil, well drained but liberally supplemented with peat moss or organic matter, is the ideal. Water liberally during hot, dry weather. Plants mature fully in 2 to 3 years. Divide *Anemone* when the plant fails to bloom well. New plants started from root cuttings or clump divisions made in early spring will bloom the same year. Pieces of root cut in fall or early spring, planted in boxes of sandy loam or leaf mulch and placed in cool greenhouses will be developed enough to be planted outdoors the following summer. If no greenhouse is available, place in a cold frame. Remove faded flowers to encourage new bloom and good plant strength. Set plants 12 to 18 inches apart when planting. The plants dislike being disturbed and shouldn't be moved unnecessarily. In Zones 5 and 6 mulch plants for winter with straw or light organic matter in fall after the ground freezes.

Uses: Cutting, middle to back of a border, naturalizing.

Recommended Varieties: Anemone 'Honorine Jobert', *A.* 'Alba', *A.* 'Queen Charlotte', *A.* 'September Charm'.

Aquilegia (ak-wil-EE-jia) columbine, Native American, light to medium shade, easy, perennial. ❦ ✳

Zones: 4 to 8 (except Florida along Gulf coast)

Height: 1½ to 3 feet depending upon variety

Colors: Blues, pinks, reds, yellows, white; most with contrasting centers

Characteristics: Columbine has been grown in gardens since the Middle Ages and appeals greatly to the imagination because of the fanciful shape of its flowers and leaves. It has graceful multicolored flowers adorned with long spurs that nod or float upright above the lacy, light green foliage, similar to that of a maidenhair fern. Each flower is made up of five petal-like sepals on top of five petals, which may be of the same or a different color. The spur is usually full of nectar and invites visits by hummingbirds. It is a short-lived perennial, lasting approximately three years in the garden. It freely self-sows if it likes its home.

Aquilegia *'McKana's Giant'*

Columbine blooms in May and June and are good companions for *Iberis* and *Dicentra*.

A. canadensis is our native woodland plant with scarlet petals and yellow centers. *A.* 'Harlequin' is an earlier blooming variety with large flowers. *A.* 'McKana's Giant' has extralarge flowers in bright colors and bicolors. *A.* 'Nora Barlow' is an unusual fully double flower of red, pink and green blooms, with no spurs. *A. flabellata*, the fan columbine, has lilac-to-white flowers.

Cultural Information: It is not difficult to grow columbine because it doesn't require any special type of soil (so long as it is reasonably fertile). It does not like moisture but needs a well-drained situation—it is even shorter lived if it doesn't have good drainage. It self-sows in favorable environments but offspring of the hybrid varieties will differ, sometimes dramatically, from the parent plants. Water generously and use an organic mulch that will feed the soil as it breaks down. Sow seeds outdoors in summer or early fall for flowering the following year. Start in a flat of sandy soil indoors 12 to 14 weeks before setting out in midspring; refrigerate the flat for 3 weeks, then place in a moist, shady spot at 70° to 75°F. Do not cover. Germination takes 3 to 4 weeks. Space plants 12 to 24 inches apart.

Uses: In a border, rock garden, bedding, background, cutting, woodland walk, naturalizing.

Recommended Varieties: Aquilegia 'McKana's Giant', *A.* 'Nora Barlow', *A.* 'Harlequin', *A. canadensis, A. flabellata.*

Aruncus (a-RUNK-us) **goatsbeard,** Native American, medium shade, easy, perennial.
Zones: 4 to 9
Height: 4 to 6 feet
Color: Cream
Characteristics: Magnificent feathery plumes of creamy blossoms appear in June and July, rising above a mass of attractive foliage like that of ferns. Bold and beautiful, *Aruncus* absolutely lights up a shady spot. It is a handsome plant that occupies a lot of space and usually looks best planted as a single specimen or at the back of a border. This moisture lover is ideal for wild gardens and near streams. *A. dioicus* is the most common. Its tall, showy blooms are ivory-white.
Cultural Information: This tall perennial rarely needs to be staked and does best in moisture-retentive soil located in lightly shaded areas. Plant about 4 feet apart as it forms large clumps and will be hard to move later. It can be divided in spring or early fall. Fertilize regularly during the growing season or use a slow-release fertilizer annually, and water generously and deeply. Set container-grown plants out in early spring.
Uses: Back of a border, accent plant, woodland walk.
Recommended: Aruncus dioicus (also known as *A. sylvester*).

Asarum (a-SAR-um) **wild ginger,** Native American, full to dense shade, easy, perennial.
Zones: 4 to 7
Height: 6 to 8 inches
Colors: Vivid green foliage, brown flowers
Characteristics: A splendid woodland perennial with glossy, round leaves. The flowers are bell shaped, brownish and drooping, and grow underneath the leaves near the ground. The flowers are incidental; no one grows wild ginger for its flowers but rather for the luxurious foliage. The common name refers to the gingery scent of the root stocks. Wild ginger is an excellent groundcover as its rhizomes spread rapidly. Also good for the wooded areas or a rock garden. *A. virginianum* is native to Virginia and the Carolinas and has dark green leaves with white spots; *A. europaeum* is hardier and easier to establish in northern climates.
Cultural Information: Plant in slightly acid soil in heavy shade with good drainage and keep moist. Plant 8 to 10 inches apart. Division is easy in spring or fall. *Asarum* can be propagated by seed with a bit more difficulty.
Uses: Groundcover, woodland garden, rock garden.
Recommended: Asarum virginianum, A. europaeum.

Asperula odorata; see *Galium odoratum*

Astilbe (as-TIL-be) **garden spirea,** light to medium shade, easy, perennial. ❦ ✳
Zones: 4 to 8
Height: 1 to 3½ feet
Colors: Pink, red, white, peach, lavender
Characteristics: This is an excellent plant for the shady border, and few can rival *Astilbe* for the grace and charm of its ferny, finely divided foliage, sometimes touched with bronze, and its feathery flower sprays.

Aruncus dioicus

Asarum europaeum

It can be combined with hosta or ferns for an easy-care groundcover or planted in a border.

A. simplicifolia 'Sprite' has cotton-candy pink plumes arching gracefully 16 inches above dark green, lacy foliage. *A. chinensis* 'Pumila' is only 12 inches high when flowering with soft lavender-pink plumes—a good edging or groundcover. *A.* ×*arendsii* 'Deutschland' sends up 18-inch white plumes that almost glow in a semishady spot or at twilight. There are many varieties to choose from and it would be difficult to make a bad decision. Plant several different varieties to extend the bloom from early July into September. The plumes are good for cutting and drying.

Cultural Information: Moist soil supplemented with peat moss or leaf mold is preferred for growing *Astilbe*. Soil must be well drained so the plant does well during its rest period in winter. *Astilbe* is a heavy feeder; feed every spring by mulching with several inches of a good organic mulch or well-rotted cow manure, and when dividing, replenish the soil before replanting. Ample water is necessary, especially during dry periods. You can cut back faded flower stalks or let them dry on the plant for added texture in the fall garden. Divide in spring or fall, when plants are three or four years old, as they multiply rapidly and exhaust the soil around them. Before resetting, replenish soil with peat moss, compost and a dusting of slow-release fertilizer. *Astilbe* can be grown from seed.

Uses: Bedding, cutting, companion plant, in front of shrubs, groundcover.

Recommended Varieties: Astilbe *simplicifolia* 'Sprite', *A. chinensis* 'Pumila', *A.* 'Deutschland'.

Autumn crocus; see ***Colchicum***

Azalea; see ***Rhododendron***

Barberry; see ***Berberis***

Barrenwort; see ***Epimedium***

Bear's-breech; see ***Acanthus***

Begonia semperflorens (beg-O-nia sem-per-FLO-renz) **fibrous begonia, wax begonia;** *Begonia tuberhybrida* (beg-O-nia too-ber-HI-bri-da) **tuberous begonia;** most are Native American from Central and South America; light, medium, full shade; challenging to grow from seed, easy from started plants; hardy annual. ❀

Zones: 4 to 10

Height: 6 to 12 inches

Colors: White, yellow, orange, pink, rose and red tones

Characteristics: There is great diversity in the foliage and flowers of the thousands of varieties of begonias. The two most popular kinds for American gardens are the wax begonia and the tuberous begonia. Green-to-bronze leaves and clusters of free-flowering, single blooms characterize the wax begonia. The tuberous begonia has large, single or double flowers that can resemble those of camellias. A very adaptable plant, the begonia remains in flower all summer and performs in all kinds of weather. It is valued as a showy plant for shady locations as well as a long-blooming potted plant. The wax begonia's green-leafed varieties usually perform better in full sun than the bronze-leafed varieties.

'Wings' begonia, a Burpee breeding breakthrough, blooms in three months or less from seed with the biggest wax begonia flowers we've seen—up to 3 inches across! The plant is bushy and base branching, growing to 10 to 12 inches and holding its flowers well above the foliage to show them off. 'Cocktail Mix' is another good variety for edging. All are good winter

Astilbe *'Rheinland'*

houseplants and cool greenhouse plants.

Tuberous begonia comes in a wide variety of colors and forms. It can be single-flowered, ruffled, full-double or camellia-form, with flowers measuring from 5 to 6½ inches across. The colors can be single or accented with a contrasting edge. There are upright growing, compact or full branched, pendulous varieties, ideal for bedding, container or hanging basket.

The Pacific Giant ruffled series and the Hanging Giant Double Hybrids were developed by three generations of leading California begonia breeders and are especially suited to American gardens. The Nonstop Hybrids are an outstanding series of compact plants with double and semidouble flowers that exhibit excellent heat tolerance, ideal for southern gardens.

Cultural Information: Both types of begonia are available from seed. If starting from seed, be careful when you open the packet. Begonia seeds are very small, and if you don't look closely you might think there are no seeds in the packet at all. Make sure your planting medium is moist and ready when you open the pack of seeds. Sow seeds on top of the planting medium and cover with a glass pane or clear plastic to keep the medium from drying out until the plants appear. They need light and heat to germinate. Growing under lights and keeping a bottom heat of 70°F helps speed germination. Seedlings have extremely fine root systems and liquid fertilizing weekly in the first few weeks before transplanting will help

Begonia semperflorens *'Vodka', 'Whiskey' and 'Gin'*

Begonia tuberhybrida *'Santa Clara'* (Pacific giant)

prevent the seedlings from starving as they quickly deplete the nutrients in the planting medium. Once established, the plants don't require weekly feeding. Growing begonia from seed is best tried by the gardener with indoor growing experience. Propagation from cuttings is easier.

Begonia can easily be propagated from leaves. Cut through several veins on the underside of a leaf and pin the leaf onto a moist planting medium. Use pins to be sure the cut veins are touching the soil. Put the container in a plastic bag to keep it moist until plants begin

to sprout at the places where the vein was cut. Three or four plants can be produced from one leaf. Once plants are established, move them to individual pots. Houseplants should be kept in a cool, light area with only a few hours of direct sunlight. Plants need repotting only when the roots fill the pot.

The tuberous varieties do best in climates with cool, damp nights. Protection from the wind and afternoon sun is essential. Soil should be rich and well drained but moisture retentive. For bloom from summer until frost, start bulbs indoors in March. Fill flats or pots with peat moss and press the bulbs into the surface. Set them in a bright spot at 72° to 80°F, and keep them evenly damp. Reduce temperature to 65°F when growth begins. When about 4 inches tall, transfer to the garden or into containers where they are to bloom, spacing them 8 to 10 inches apart. In fall, when the leaves turn yellow and begin to drop, lift the bulbs, remove the stems and store the bulbs in a cool, dry place until time to replant them in the spring. Wax begonia is one of the few flowers that bloom under almost any light conditions, but it does best in light shade. It blooms continuously all summer and is rarely damaged by wind, rain or pests. Space 6 to 8 inches apart.

Uses: Edging, bedding, houseplant, rock garden, container plant.

Recommended Varieties: All wax begonia and tuberous begonia, notably the Nonstop Hybrids, Pacific Giant Double Hybrids, 'Wings' and 'Cocktail Mix'.

Bellflower; see *Campanula*

Berberis (BER-ber-is) **barberry,** light, medium, full shade, easy, shrub.

Zones: 5 to 8, depending on variety

Height: 4 to 5 feet

Colors: Bright yellow flowers in spring, bright red or blue-black berries in fall

Characteristics: The barberry shrub makes an excellent hedge. It is upright with thorny branches and thick leaves that form an impenetrable barrier. Each species of the barberry develops low-growing plants with green foliage. The leaves are lighter underneath, lustrous green on top. The small, golden yellow spring flowers develop into fruits in the fall. Most have brilliant fall color.

Berberis Thunbergii, the Japanese barberry, is considered one of the best deciduous hedge plants. Its scarlet berries remain on the plant for an extended period, sometimes lasting through the winter. This is the best one for shade and poor soils. *B.* ×*mentorensis* is recommended for the Midwest as it is tolerant of the dry summers. This same variety remains evergreen in the Southwest. There are also a crimson variety and a golden variety.

Cultural Information: Barberry is undemanding and will tolerate most kinds of soils and situations except waterlogged soils. Plant uniformly in rows 15 to 18 inches apart for hedges. It grows to 4 feet in three years.

Uses: Along walk, foundation, hedge.

Recommended: Berberis Thunbergii, B. ×*mentorensis.*

Bergenia (ber-GEN-ia) **megasea** or **saxifraga,** medium to full shade, easy, perennial.

🌑 💧

Zones: 4 to 8

Height: 12 to 18 inches

Colors: Bright pink, white

Characteristics: Bergenia is grown for its large, glossy, leathery leaves that turn bronze to dark red in cold weather. The

Bergenia cordifolia

Berberis Thunbergii

edges are scalloped and wavy. In spring large clusters of bright pink flowers appear on short, sturdy stems that barely extend above the leaves. *B. cordifolia* produces handsome, lavender-pink blooms; *B.* 'Alba' produces white. Both the foliage and the flowers are used in arrangements; flowers last long when cut. The foliage remains green year 'round in southern regions; it doesn't die back in northern climates, and although it can look untidy by spring, it is quickly replaced by new green leaves.

Cultural Information: Bergenia likes a well-drained, almost stony soil but will accept a wide range of moisture conditions. Grows slowly in dry areas, rapidly in such constantly wet spots as beside a brook or pool. Remove faded flowers. Divide after three or four years of flowering to prevent overcrowding. It needs lime and prefers gritty or sandy soil. Give it protection from the noonday sun.

Uses: Edging, cutting, groundcover.

Recommended Varieties: Bergenia cordifolia, B. cordifolia 'Alba'.

Bishop's hat; see ***Epimedium***

Bleeding heart; see ***Dicentra***

Bluebells, Spanish; see ***Endymion***

Bluebells, Virginia; see ***Mertensia***

Blue cardinal flower; see ***Lobelia***

Browallia (brow-WALL-ia) **sapphire flower,** Native American from Colombia, easy, half-hardy annual. ❀

Height: 9 to 10 inches

Colors: Shades of blue, white, lavender

Characteristics: This annual or tender perennial plant has small terminal clusters of blue star-shaped flowers that cover the plant in a branching habit. The leaves are bright green and pointed. Grown as annuals in most places, they can't tolerate temperatures lower than 40° to 45°F. Best known for its blue varieties, *Browallia* in lavenders and white is very attractive. The branching habit makes it nice for hanging baskets.

B. speciosa 'Blue Bells Improved' has violet-blue flowers (1 to 2 inches across) that turn lavender-blue and require no pinching to stay bushy. *B. speciosa* 'Jingle Bells' comes in shades of blue, white and lavender. *B. speciosa* 'Silver Bells' is a lovely mixture of white and blue shades.

Cultural Information: The seeds need light to germinate; don't cover with soil. During summer, pinch back to maintain neat shape and encourage flowering. If growing *Browallia* in a container, keep its roots snug, or pot-bound, and be careful not to overfeed and overwater or you will have leaves and no flowers. It likes high humidity and suffers in hot, dry air. A daily misting will be greatly appreciated. This plant often self-sows in protected beds or warmer climates. Space 6 to 8 inches apart. Start indoors 8 to 10 weeks before last frost.

Uses: Hanging basket, container plant, in a border.

Recommended Varieties: Browallia speciosa 'Blue Bells Improved', *B. speciosa* 'Jingle Bells', *B. speciosa* 'Silver Bells'.

Brunnera macrophylla
(BRUNN-er-a mack-ro-FEEL-ya) **perennial forget-me-not,** light shade, easy, perennial.

Zones: 3 to 9

Height: 12 to 18 inches

Color: Blue

Characteristics: An exquisite dwarf perennial with airy sprays of small, intense, true blue flowers rising above the foliage. It has a dense, mounded habit and handsome, round, textured leaves of cool green. *Brunnera* makes an effective groundcover even when not in bloom; try in woodlands, interplant with late-blooming tulips or use as contrast

Brunnera macrophylla

Browallia *'Blue Bells Improved'*

for spring-blooming shrubs. *Cultural Information:* Deeply prepared, moist soils, well drained and of medium texture, are best. Watering is necessary during hot, dry periods. Foliage and clump size will be much smaller in dry, shady sites. It seeds itself prolifically and can be grown untended as if wild in wooded areas. It's a good choice for the middle of a shaded border. Planting may be done in spring or fall. Set plants 12 to 18 inches apart. To prevent crowding, divide clumps in the early spring after the second or third year of flowering. Root cuttings may be taken in the early spring. Remove faded flowers

Caladium 'Irene Dank'

Caladium 'Candidum'

to encourage new growth. To sow seed in early spring, freeze it for one week, then plant outdoors at 75°F. It will take two weeks to germinate. Most diseases can be avoided by not overwatering plants, spacing plants well for good air circulation and keeping weeds cleaned out of the garden.

Uses: Cutting, companion plant, groundcover, woodland.

Bugbane; see ***Cimicifuga***

Bugleweed; see ***Ajuga***

Bunchberry; see ***Cornus***

Busy lizzy; see ***Impatiens***

Caladium (kal-AY-dium) **mother-in-law plant,** medium, full, dense shade, easy, bulb/ tuber. 💧

Zones: Zone 10, outdoors year 'round; Zones 3 to 9, start indoors two months before temperature will remain a constant 70°F

Height: 12 inches

Colors: White, pinks, reds

Characteristics: Caladium is grown for its large arrowhead- or heart-shaped, veined leaves tinted with shades of green, silver, white, rose or red. Excellent for dense shade, it comes in a variety of textures and patterns. It is perfect for southern climates because it thrives in summer heat. There are fancy-leafed and lance-leafed caladiums, the only difference being the shape of the leaf—fancy-leafed is more heart-shaped, lance-leafed is more arrowhead-shaped. It comes in dozens of

colors, patterns and combinations that range from the white to deep red. *Caladium* 'Candidum' is white with green veins, *C*. 'Pink Symphony' is pink with green veins and *C*. 'Gypsy Rose' is a deep, rosy color. Many catalogs offer mixed colors but it is usually a good idea to avoid these and opt instead for massing a single type or limit yourself to two carefully selected colors. Using two or more colors requires careful planning.

Cultural Information: Caladium is a tuber. Notice the difference in sizes when purchasing tubers. They are 1 to 3 inches long and priced accordingly. The larger the tuber, the greater amount of foliage you can expect. A few large ones can create much the same effect as six to eight smaller ones. Plant 12 inches apart in soil that is evenly moist, and water if it doesn't rain. It cannot remain outdoors over winter except in Zone 10. In Zones 3 to 9, start the tubers two months before the temperature will remain above 70°F, in a mixture of equal parts of loam, coarse sand and peat moss with ½ teaspoon 5-10-5 fertilizer added for each 4-inch potful of mix. Place the tuber in a pot with the knobby side up and cover with 1 to 2 inches of mix. Keep damp until growth is active, then keep soil moist. Plant outside only when the soil is warm, in May (Mother's Day in Zone 6B). Can be planted directly outside after all danger of frost. Continue to fertilize each month during the growing season. In the fall, lift with a clump of soil, compress gently and set to dry in a frost-free, shaded spot. This usually takes no more than a day or two. Cut off dried foliage and store in a moderately warm basement. To propagate, divide tuberous roots several days before replanting. Watch for slugs.

Uses: In a border, bedding, container plant, background, accent plant.

Recommended Varieties: Caladum 'Candidum', _C._ 'Pink Symphony', _C._ 'Gypsy Rose', _C._ 'Irene Dank'.

Camellia (kam-EEL-ya) **common camellia,** light to medium shade, easy in Zones 8 to 10 (can be grown in pots in the North), shrub.

Zones: 7 to 10
Height: 6 to 12 feet but may reach 20 feet
Colors: White, red, pink
Characteristics: Camellia has been a treasured plant among southerners for more than 150 years. And try as we might, most varieties of these shrubs are very difficult to grow in the cooler climates of the North unless planted in a location sheltered from summer sun and winter cold. It thrives on the West Coast and in southern states. It is a glossy, evergreen bush densely foliaged with shiny leaves and covered with brilliant flowers. It is worth growing camellia for foliage alone, but the flowers are exquisite. They begin blooming in midfall and some peak in early spring. Later-blooming varieties continue into midspring.

C. japonica is the common camellia, the hardiest and most widely grown. The flowers are large, waxy and usually white, but many cultivars feature pink,

red or variegated blossoms; they bloom from October to April. They come in both double and semidouble form. _C._ 'Purity' has large, double white flowers of the sort used for corsages; _C._ 'Kumasaka' is a variegated double; _C._ 'Professor C. S. Sargent' is a red variety and one of the hardiest; _C._ 'Mathotiana' is another double red, larger than 'Professor C. S. Sargent'.

Cultural Information: Camellia is an excellent partially (medium) shaded plant. It will tolerate some sun along the Gulf Coast; however, in northern areas, protect from sun until well established to prevent the roots from drying out. It is widely grown from North Carolina southward and on the Pacific Coast from California to Vancouver, B.C. Plant in acid soil and keep evenly moist. It is a slow grower unless well cultivated and fed. In areas where there is danger of frost, add a permanent mulch of wood chips. Prune in spring after flowering. Propagate by rooting stem cuttings in midsummer. The plant is shallow rooted, so don't cultivate around the roots.

Uses: Hedge, accent plant, along wall.

Recommended Varieties: Camellia japonica, C. 'Kumasaka', _C._ 'Mathotiana', _C._ 'Professor C. S. Sargent', _C._ 'Purity', _C._ 'David Reed'.

Campanula (kam-PAN-yoo-la) **bellflower,** light shade, easy, biennial and perennial. ❀ ❚

Zones: 3 to 9
Height: 6 inches to 4 feet
Colors: Blue, purple, white
Characteristics: The name _Campanula_ as well as the shape of

the flowers immediately bring to mind a bell, hence the common name. The genus _Campanula_ consists of about 300 species and they come in every size imaginable from the tiny _C. carpatica_ to the stately cup-and-saucer _C. Medium_ (the biennial commonly called Canterbury bells). Mostly in shades of blue and purple, with an occasional white variety, the flowers are bell shaped, some nodding, some looking up. The shorter varieties tend to be more long lived than the taller ones. _C. carpatica_ has cuplike blue flowers; low-growing and vigorous, reliable and charming, it has long been a favorite, blooming from June to September. _C. glomerata_ has clustered purple-blue, bell-shaped flowers. _C. persicifolia_ has erect flowers on short stalks that form a loose cluster rising from a central axis, and is a popular cut flower in Europe. _C. rotundifolia_, the bluebell of Scotland, features nodding, bright blue flowers on slender stems.

Cultural Information: Campanula is not difficult to cultivate, adaptable to any ordinary garden soil but will perform better with richer soils. Provide ample water during the blooming period. All can be grown from seed one summer to flower the next. It is also easy to propagate by division. The smaller the plants, the more you need to mass them for good garden display. The only real problems are slugs and snails.

Uses: Bedding, rock garden, in a border, cutting.

Recommended: Campanula Medium, C. carpatica, C. glomerata, C. persicifolia.

Camellia japonica
'David Reed'

Campanula glomerata

Ceratostigma plumb-aginoides

Chelone Lyonii

Chrysogonum virginia-num 'Allen Bush'

Cardinal flower; see *Lobelia*

Ceratostigma plumba-ginoides (ser-at-oh-STIG-ma plom-bag-in-OY-decz) **leadwort or plumbago,** light shade, easy, perennial.
Zones: 5 to 9
Height: 9 to 12 inches
Colors: Deep cobalt blue, violet
Characteristics: This charming plant has attractive bronze-red leaves in fall and beautiful blue flowers in late summer and fall. This is a creeping perennial whose flowers will bloom in full sun, but afternoon shade will result in open plants that spread more freely. It is certainly a plant that deserves to be planted more frequently. Makes an excellent overplanting for early bulbs like crocuses. It is a native of China, where it was found on the walls of Peking.
Cultural Information: Growth is slow to start in spring, but is quicker in summer. It is a long-lived perennial and should be planted in moist soil with light shade. Tends to be vigorous and should be watched once it is established. Best planted in spring, which is also the best time for propagation. Lift the plants and separate for replanting. Cuttings may be taken in summer, placed in a sandy soil, and covered and stored.
Uses: Groundcover, accent plant.

Chelone (kell-O-nee) **pink turtlehead,** Native American, light to medium shade, easy, perennial.
Zones: 4 to 9
Height: 2 to 4 feet
Colors: Pink, white, rose, purple
Characteristics: This rarely seen plant is unusual and eye-catching. It is an excellent woodland plant, clothed in glossy green foliage. In late summer and early fall, it bears short spikes of pink, hooded flowers that indeed resemble the heads of turtles, hence the common name. Because it blooms in late summer, it is good to grow during the period between summer flowers and asters. *C. Lyonii* is the most common, and a lovely pink variety with dark green sawtooth, pointed leaves. Tip-pinching the plant will make for a bushier habit. *C. obliqua* is a red turtlehead with slightly narrower leaves, and is somewhat less hardy. *C. Lyonii* isn't happy much south of Zone 7; *C. obliqua* is more heat tolerant in Zones 6 to 9.
Cultural Information: Plant in moisture-retentive soil, rich with organic matter, and it will require little maintenance. Divide every few years as it spreads rapidly. Leave the dead stems over winter, and remove them in spring. May need support in exposed positions. A summer mulch helps keep the roots cool and moist, what the plant prefers. Propagation can be by division, cutting and seed.

Uses: Back of a border, woodland walk, bog garden, bank of a stream.
Recommended: Chelone Lyonii, *C. obliqua.*

Christmas rose; see *Helleborus*

Chrysogonum virginia-num (kris-OG-o-num vir-gin-ee-AY-num) **goldenstar,** Native American, light, medium, full shade, easy, perennial. ✿
Zones: 5 to 9
Height: 4 to 8 inches
Color: Yellow
Characteristics: A truly wonderful groundcover, this plant is found in woods from Pennsylvania and West Virginia to Florida and Louisiana. Its popularity has grown so much over recent years that nurseries have had trouble keeping up with demand. *Chrysogonum* is low growing with bright golden flowers and handsome, glossy green foliage. Many catalogs state that it blooms from May until October, but I have never found this to be true; in my experience it blooms in May and June. The *C. virginianum* 'Allen Bush' is said to bloom longer. It spreads rapidly by means of rhizomes and has a loose, open habit that looks particularly nice among rocks; it is not invasive.
Cultural Information: Plant in a mixture of rich organic soil with sand for good drainage—critical for this plant. The soil should be slightly moist and doesn't need much fertilizing (too much fertilizing will result in fewer flowers). In southern climates it can be planted in heavier shade.
Uses: Groundcover, rock garden, woodland.

Cimicifuga (sim-i-siff-EW-ga) **bugbane, fairy candles,** Native American, medium to full shade, moderately easy, perennial.
Zones: 3 to 8
Height: 3 to 6 feet
Color: White
Characteristics: An excellent plant for lighting up those dark, shady areas, *Cimicifuga* is a graceful woodland plant that sends tall, feathery white jets well up above the foliage. Glowing at dusk, they resemble fairy candles. The elegant spires of tiny white flowers bloom on *C. racemosa* from July through August and are admirably suited as companions for monkshood. Plant *C. simplex* 'White Pearl' for late September and October bloom. It is very showy planted in front of shrubs, especially with the red berries of some *Viburnum* species. A highly recommended plant for the shade garden.
Cultural Information: Cimicifuga requires moisture-retentive, slightly acid soil rich in organic matter. To plant bare-root clumps from a division, place rhizome or rootstock (with at least two

eyes) so that the eyes are 1 inch below soil level. To sow seeds in spring, prechill them in the refrigerator for several weeks before planting, then sow at 70° to 75°F. Germination is slow and erratic, best when seed is fresh. The common name bugbane may have been given because they are not bothered by insect pests and only rarely by disease.
Uses: In a border, woodland walk, shady nook.
Recommended Varieties: Cimicifuga racemosa, C. 'White Pearl'.

Clematis (KLEM-a-tis), light to medium shade, easy to moderate, perennial vine.
Zones: 3 to 9
Height: 3 feet for *C. heracleifolia;* large-flowered hybrids, 8 to 20 feet; small-flowering species to 30 feet
Colors: Blue, white, pink, red, bicolor
Characteristics: Clematis is the most beautiful of all hardy flowering vines. It has immense, perfect blooms up to 6 inches and creates a profusion of blooms during late spring and summer. Use it on a trellis, arbor or

pergola, let it climb on a fence or frame a doorway. You can also use other plants for its supports—growing up trees, over shrubs and among and over your climbing roses. Clematis can make a flowering shrub appear to be in bloom when it is not; for example, forsythia—which blooms in the early spring—could be covered with *Clematis × Jackmanii*'s large, deep purple flowers from June to September. Other popular large-flowered hybrids are *C.* 'Ernest Markham', with ruby-red blooms; *C.* 'Lincoln Star', with large, pointed flowers of raspberry-pink with lavender edges and dark stamens and *C.* 'Will Goodwin', with large, 6- to-8-inch pure blue flowers adorned with golden stamens.

The species types are smaller flowered than the hybrids, but grow taller with a profusion of flowers. *C. maximowicziana*, widely known as *C. paniculata*, is the sweet autumn clematis. The vigorous vines grow to 30 feet, blooming in September and October with a profusion of 1-inch white flowers deliciously scented like hawthorne. The flowers are followed by silvery seed heads that are wonderful for winter arrangements. *C.* 'Vyvan Pennell' is light purple with dark purple edges. *C. heracleifolia* is a vine not like most familiar clematis, but is rather a bushy perennial, growing 3 feet and clothed in attractive, divided foliage. The flowers, appearing in late summer, are rich blue, borne in clusters, and somewhat resemble hyacinths, including a delightful fragrance.
Cultural Information: Clematis needs to receive sun at its top

Cimicifuga racemosa

Clematis × Jackmanii

Cleome 'Queen Mixed'

and shade at its roots, the latter provided either by a groundcover or a mulch. Soil should be very high in organic content, well drained but moisture retentive. Plant them at least 2 feet from any structure. If you'd like a vine to grow up a tree or a shrub, plant the vine under the outside circumference of the tree or shrub. The vine will easily be able to grow into and over the shrub, but for the tree you'll need to train it up a heavy string or wire to the lower branches, and from there it can find its own way. Water during periods of drought and fertilize and replenish the soil by mulching with compost, wood chips, pine needles or shredded leaf mulch. Some gardeners recommend putting a flat, 12-inch stone near the vine to make sure the soil stays cool and damp on the roots. Don't incorporate chemical fertilizer into the soil as it could burn the roots. Clematis may take some time to start top growth; they must first establish their roots in their new home. Plant about 4 feet apart.

Clethra alnifolia

Recommended Varieties: Clematis heracleifolia, C. × Jackmanii, C. 'Ernest Markham', C. 'Lincoln Star', C. 'Will Goodwin', C. maximowicziana, C. 'Vyvan Pennell'.

Cleome (klee-O-mee) spider plant, tropical Native American, light to medium shade, easy, annual. 🌡 ❀ 💧

Height: 3 to 5 feet
Colors: White, pinks, purple, burgundy
Characteristics: A very attractive, tall, weather-resistant plant, *Cleome* is excellent for backgrounds, large accents, floral screens and hedges. Its seedpods develop and dangle, like spider legs, under the big, airy flower clusters. The flowers are haloed by an outer circle of long, graceful stamens. On bright sunny days, the flower petals will curl up, opening again as evening approaches. But when this showy free-flowering plant is kept out of direct sun, the petals stay open all the time.

When grown in a row, the plants create a temporary hedge 3 feet wide, useful for screening an unsightly area. If planted at the back of a small garden, four plants are enough to cover an area 9 × 3 feet. Plants are leafless and leggy at the bottom so it is best to plant in front of them. When cutting for bouquets, be careful of thorns located at every place where a flowering branch joins the stem. The leaves and stems are sticky to the touch. The flowers have a lemony fragrance. *Cleome* 'Pink Queen', C. hasslevana 'Purple Queen' and C. 'Helen Campbell' all produce large, airy

flowers. C. lutea, the yellow bee plant, is a Native American annual from California and Colorado.
Cultural Information: This plant tolerates heat and drought and performs well when direct sown outside after all danger of frost. It sets seeds easily. The seedpods form directly under the flower while the flower is still blooming; they add interest and need not be removed. You can remove faded flowers to help the plant branch and produce more flowers. However, *Cleome* is long flowering even while prolifically producing seed. Whether or not you cut off spent flowers, the plants will bloom until killed by prolonged frost. Each individual flower lasts for several weeks. These plants frequently reseed, but the seedlings may revert in color and be weedy looking. It can be grown next to a fence to which stems can be tied if support is needed. *Cleome* should be spaced 2 feet apart. It is not easily bothered by pests or disease.
Uses: Back of a border, cutting, temporary hedge or shrub.
Recommended Varieties: Cleome 'Pink Queen', C. hasslevana 'Purple Queen', C. 'Helen Campbell', C. lutea.

Clethra (KLETH-ra) sweet pepperbush or pink summer sweet, Native American, light shade, difficult to establish, shrub.

Zones: 4 to 9
Height: 4 to 6 feet
Colors: White, pink
Characteristics: Summer sweet is a common shrub of the eastern United States. Blooming in July and August, it features

shiny leaves 1½ to 4 inches long that turn yellow, and in some cases orange, in fall. It forms thick foliage and is sometimes sheared as a hedge. *Clethra* tolerates wind and salty sea air and will thrive in wet soil, making this an excellent plant for a seashore garden. *C. alnifolia* has very fragrant white spikes in July. *C. alnifolia* 'Rosea' has a lovely pink flower.

Cultural Information: Clethra will thrive in almost any soil but is particularly useful in difficult, wet areas of the garden. It does best in moist, acid soil high in organic matter. Plant container-grown plants in early spring and water abundantly. When pruning is necessary, do so in early spring. Clip off faded flowers to stimulate new growth, though seed heads are attractive in fall and winter. Propagate additional plants from cuttings of new wood taken in late spring or early summer, or in mid-fall from hardened stems. *Clethra* is pest free and will attract many bees while in flower.

Uses: Back of a border, cutting.
Recommended Varieties: Clethra alnifolia, C. alnifolia 'Rosea', *C. barbinervis* 'Japanese Clethra'.

Climbing hydrangea; see *Hydrangea*

Colchicum (KOL-chi-kum) autumn crocus, light to medium shade, easy, bulb.

Zones: 4 to 10
Height: Up to 9 inches
Colors: Rosy purple, white
Characteristics: Called the autumn crocus, colchicum is a hardy bulb that is a charming plant with crocuslike flowers that bloom in fall. It has unusually

large, broad leaves that appear in early spring. This plant tends to take up room in the spring when the leaves are developing; plant it among low-growing, carpeting plants or in the grass. It is best grown in masses or naturalized among low-growing groundcovers, where it provides a welcome splash of color in fall. The chief varieties are *Colchicum autumnale,* bearing lovely lilac-rose flowers during September, and *C. speciosum,* with unusually large, deep lavender flowers. *C. speciosum* 'Album' is a white variety, and *C.* 'The Giant' has large goblets of rich lilac-pink.

Cultural Information: Plant in August or September in well-drained, fertile soil with shade from early leaf-losing trees and good reflected light, and cover bulb 4 inches. Plant 6 inches apart. For division, bulbs may be lifted as soon as the leaves have died down, separated and replanted immediately.

Uses: Under a groundcover.
Recommended Varieties: Colchicum autumnale, C. speciosum 'Album', *C.* 'The Giant'.

Coleus (KO-le-us) foliage plant, light to medium shade, moderately easy, annual.

Zones: 3 to 10
Height: 12 to 21 inches
Colors: White, cream, greens, pinks, reds, scarlets, browns, oranges, combined in multicolor or bicolor foliage.
Characteristics: Coleus turns shady areas into kaleidoscopes of color with bold, bright, multicolor and bicolor foliage combinations. It is excellent for striking accents, as a

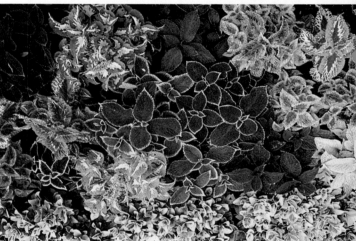

background for low-growing annuals or for an Oriental carpet groundcover. Use it to beautify the north or east side of your house, under trees or shrubs or on shady patios or porches.

There are several different varieties of coleus with different leaf sizes and shapes, varying from tapered or small lobed to large fringed, heart shaped and lobed. The richly colored leaves are often deeply cut or toothed around the edges. Coleus thrives in pots, baskets and other containers. In winter, it can be grown indoors as a houseplant.

The whorls of small blue and lavender flowers held in spikes are insignificant and should be

Top: Colchicum *species*

Above: Coleus *species*

removed to prevent the plant from going to seed and to encourage the growth of more foliage. The flowers at the bottom of the spike sprout into seedpods first, dangling like spider legs from the stem. The Wizard Series forms neat, compact, base-branching plants with large, heart-shaped leaves. The beauty of this series is that the plants don't need to be pinched back. The Carefree Series stays dwarf and very bushy all season. The oaklike, lobed foliage is smaller than most with amber, brown and bronzy scarlet, plus cool green, ivory and rich mahogany crimson.

Cultural Information: Sow indoors six to eight weeks before the last expected spring frost for summer gardens. Coleus needs a little light during germination. Keep seedlings and plants moist during the growing season. The young seedlings will be green, developing their colorful foliage as they mature. Mulch will help both garden and potted plants stay moist.

Cuttings made in late summer are so easy to grow they can be rooted in water and potted up for indoor plants and gifts for friends. Seeds can be sown any time for indoor houseplants. Pinch back new growth to induce bushiness. Coleus grows well in any good, well-drained soil. The colors are more vivid when grown in medium shade. Space plants 8 to 10 inches apart.

Uses: Groundcover, in a border, container plant, window box, houseplant.

Recommended Varieties: Coleus Wizard Series, *C*. Carefree Series.

Convallaria *species*

Columbine; see *Aquilegia*

Common camellia; see *Camellia*

Convallaria (kon-val-AIR-ia) **lily of the valley,** Native American, full to dense shade, easy, perennial. ◖

Zones: 3 to 9
Height: 3 to 8 inches
Colors: White, pink
Characteristics: This old and beloved garden favorite has delicate bell-like flowers that are very fragrant. The ¼-inch flowers appear in midspring, followed by orange berries. It makes an excellent groundcover for particularly shady spots. In dense shade, a carpet of leaves will thrive but there will be fewer flowers. The plant increases rapidly (by underground stems called "pips"), needs minimum care, is long lived and is rarely invasive. *C. majalis* 'Rosea' is a handsome pink.

Cultural Information: Convallaria can be grown under almost any conditions but performs best in the cooler zones and with

rich, moist, acid soil. Best results are obtained by an application of compost, manure or other organic fertilizer each year in the fall.

Uses: Woodland, under trees, edging, groundcover.

Recommended Varieties: Convallaria majalis, C. majalis 'Rosea'.

Coralbells; see *Heuchera*

Cornus canadensis (KOR-nus kan-ah-DEN-sis) **bunchberry,** Native American, medium to full shade, challenging, perennial. ◖

Zones: 2 to 7
Height: 5 to 9 inches
Color: White
Characteristics: This delightful little evergreen is a familiar sight in the mountains of eastern North America but can be slow to get established in the garden. It's worth the effort, for once established it spreads rapidly on creeping underground stems. The dainty, crinkled leaves are 3 inches long, and the tiny greenish flowers have

Cornus canadensis

four to six white petals. It flowers in late spring or early summer, followed by bright red, edible berries in late summer and fall. This is a particularly useful plant for a woodland setting.

Cultural Information: The soil is most important. It must be acid, cool, humus, boglike soil rich in sphagnum moss. Plant bunchberry in spring or fall in groups of at least three or in drifts, spacing them about 12 inches apart. Keep the ground cool and moist by a mulch of pine needles. Sow seeds in fall to germinate in spring; sowing seeds is challenging. Plants should not be collected from the wild. They are difficult to establish and should be left undisturbed.

Uses: Woodland, groundcover, under trees and shrubs.

Corydalis (ko-RY-dal-is) **yellow corydalis,** Native American, medium to dense shade, easy, perennial. ❀

Zones: 5 to 7
Height: 9 to 15 inches
Colors: Yellow, purple
Characteristics: Corydalis has never been a popular garden favorite and that's puzzling, considering that it is easy and hardy, grows in shade or sun and has few pest problems. Part of its problem is that it is not easy to find, but it is worth seeking out.

Corydalis aurea and *C. sempervirens* are the two Native American species. Both have yellow cone-shaped flowers with one spur. *C. aurea* is low growing and spreads nicely—but not invasively. *C. lutea* is a European native, and referred to

commonly as the yellow corydalis. It is also the one most readily available in the trade. Often called the yellow bleeding heart, *C. lutea* has four-petaled flowers on bushy stems. The flowers are borne on spikes above the finely divided, fernlike foliage. It has a long bloom period, from May through August in most areas. The *C. lutea* should be grown more frequently than it is for its long-lasting blooms and foliage that remains intact for most of the season. (The foliage alone make this plant worth growing.) It grows best in medium to full shade but will also tolerate dense shade.

Cultural Information: Plant 8 inches apart in well-drained soil and supplement the soil with compost and other organic matter. Readily self-sows. Fertilize each spring. Propagate from seeds, division or from cuttings taken in summer. Transplant only in spring.

Uses: In a border, against a wall, rock garden, arrangement.

Recommended: Corydalis aurea, C. sempervirens, C. lutea.

Cranesbill; see *Geranium*

Creeping myrtle; see *Vinca*

Crocus (KRO-kus) light to medium shade, easy, bulb.

Zones: 3 to 9
Height: 3 to 6 inches
Colors: Violet, lilac, pinkish purple, lavender-blue, white, yellow, striped bicolors
Characteristics: Crocus is the most familiar sign of spring. This small bulb comes in a brilliant variety of colors and is most

effective when massed. It naturalizes nicely in grass or with shrubbery. There are many varieties of crocus, some spring bloomers and some fall bloomers. It has a dainty little flower that is deeply colored.

Cultural Information: Crocus needs some sun, but unless your shade is under evergreens or beside a building, plant away because crocus blooms early enough—before the deciduous trees leaf-out—to catch some rays. Best in sandy or well-drained soil; avoid very damp situations. Use Bulb Booster or bone meal when you plant and

Corydalis lutea

Top: Crocus ancyrensis
'Golden Bunch'

Above: Crocus 'Blue
Ribbon'

leave for several years. Planting bulbs close to deciduous shrubs helps as a buffer against rabbits. Cover the bulbs about 3 inches. If left alone in good soil it will multiply rapidly. Be careful when you mow—its leaves must die off naturally or the flowers will not return.

Uses: Groundcover, naturalizing, woodland, under trees.

Recommended Varieties: Crocus speciosus, C. Kotschyanus, C. medius, C. laevigatus, Dutch Hybrids 'Giant Purple', 'Snowstorm' and Royalty Dutch Crocus Mixture.

Crocus, autumn; see *Colchicum*

Daffodil; see *Narcissus*

Dame's rocket; see *Hesperis*

Daylily; see *Hemerocallis*

Dead nettle; see *Lamium*

Dicentra (dy-SEN-tra) **bleeding heart,** Native American, light to medium shade, moderately easy, perennial. 🔔 ✿ 💧

Zones: 3 to 9

Height: 1 to 2½ feet; 10 to 12 inches for dwarf varieties

Colors: Pink, red, white

Characteristics: This old-fashioned favorite derives its common name from the heart shape of the flowers. A favorite of gardeners for years, *D. spectabilis* grows hardily with rather long stalks of pink flowers on 2-foot plants. Its attractive ornamental foliage will remain in good condition all summer provided the plant is not allowed to dry out excessively. If grown in full sun its foliage will disappear shortly after flowering. Particularly at home in the woodland garden, it boasts graceful, compound leaves with arching stems that hold the flowers. Especially beautiful in the midst of late-season tulips, it lends an airiness to the spring garden. It goes dormant and dies back to the roots late in summer, to emerge once again in all its glory the following year.

D. eximia, the fringed bleeding heart, is dwarf, 10 to 12 inches, and flowers off and on all summer. It makes a soft groundcover and provides flowers for cutting. *D. eximia* 'Alba' has pure white flowers that start in late spring and continue all summer. *Dicentra* self-sows.

Cultural Information: This plant likes humus-rich, well-drained soil in partial shade. Plant in early fall or early spring and leave undisturbed. Water and feed regularly but cut back when dormant period begins. Because bleeding heart lasts for years, it will probably become overcrowded and need dividing in three to four years. Dig up in early spring but be sure to handle the roots very carefully because they are extremely brittle. Each piece of root division should have an eye or bud, but the root itself need not be more than 3 inches long. New planting locations should be well marked to protect any early growth or dormant roots from cultivation accidents. For continuous blooming all summer of *D. eximia,* remove the spent blossoms regularly. It is easiest to purchase young plants from the nursery or from the Burpee catalog before new growth begins in spring.

Space 2 feet apart, and if planting in rows, space rows 3 feet apart. It can be started from seed but this requires a lot of patience.

Uses: In a border, rock garden, woodland walk, groundcover.

Recommended Varieties: Dicentra spectabilis, D. eximia, D. eximia 'Alba'.

Digitalis (dij-it-AY-lis) **foxglove,** medium shade, easy, biennial, perennial. 🔔 ✿ 💧

Zones: 4 to 9

Height: 3 to 5 feet

Colors: Purple, pink, white, red, yellow, bicolors

Characteristics: One of the loveliest of garden flowers, foxglove is so named because the flowers look like the fingers of a glove. It is a tall, stately plant, with spikes of speckled blooms. Excellent at the rear of a border or in a woodland walk, foxglove blooms in late spring and early summer. The light green leaves form a low rosette, evergreen in all but the coldest climates. Most foxgloves, however, are not perennial but biennial, and establish large clumps because they self-sow freely. *D. × mertonensis* is a truly perennial foxglove, only 3 feet tall but bearing spikes of bell-shaped flowers the color of strawberry ice cream. *D. purpurea* 'Excelsior' is a biennial with superior, large flowers borne horizontally all around the stem rather than the usual pendant blooms on three sides. *D. purpurea* 'Foxy' is the only foxglove that will bloom from seed the first year, approximately five months from sowing.

Cultural Information: Foxglove

Dicentra spectabilis

Digitalis purpurea

is best grown in well-drained yet moisture-retentive soil, rich in leaf mold or other organic matter, and spaced 1 foot apart. Plant nursery plants in the spring or fall. Sow seed outdoors in late spring or early summer for flowers the following spring. They can be started indoors at 70°F and will germinate in one to three weeks. Taller varieties will probably need staking. If the flower stalks are cut back after flowering they might bloom again in the fall. If you want the plant to reseed by itself, leave at least one stalk standing. Transplant seedlings in late summer. Protect with salt hay or other winter mulch in northern climates. Foliage is poisonous if eaten.
Uses: Back of a border, woodland walk.
Recommended Varieties: Digitalis × mertonensis, D. purpurea 'Excelsior', *D. purpurea* 'Foxy'.

Dodecatheon (do-dec-ATH-eon) shooting star, Native American, medium shade, difficult, perennial.

Zones: 3 to 9, depending on variety
Height: 18 inches
Color: Rose-purple
Characteristics: This is a plant only for the passionate, experienced gardener. In bloom this flower is like a fireworks display, the blossoms in subtle colors nodding on their long stalks. They have a short life cycle of only three months—flowering April to June—and die back in winter. *Dodecatheon Meadia,* the common shooting star, is a wonderful addition to any garden if you are willing to give it a little extra time. This plant grows from

Pennsylvania to Georgia to Texas.
Cultural Information: Enrich soil with peat and leaf mold. The soil should be rich in organic matter and be able to hold enough water to feed the plant right through spring. *Dodecatheon* needs moisture during the growing season and dry conditions when dormant. Let clumps fill out before dividing in September. Plant 8 inches apart in early fall and in March.
Uses: Woodland, deep soil pockets in rock garden.
Recommended: Dodecatheon Meadia.

Dog-tooth violet; see Erythronium

Doronicum (do-RON-ik-um) leopard's bane, sun, medium shade, easy, perennial.

Zones: 3 to 8
Height: 2 to 4 feet
Color: Yellow
Characteristics: These bright yellow, daisylike flowers make an excellent addition to the garden. This early bloomer is a favorite combined with May-blooming tulips and Virginia bluebells. The handsome, heart-shaped green leaves provide the perfect foil for the 2-inch golden daisies so freely produced in spring, and the blooms on long stems are fine for cutting.
Cultural Information: Should be set out in rich, moisture-retentive soil. Plant dies back, going dormant in July or August (label it so you don't mistakenly disturb it) and should be watered even during that period. Best when nursery plants or divisions taken in late August are used. Sow seeds outdoors in late spring or

early summer. Germination will be slow and erratic, taking up to four weeks.
Uses: Cuttings, border, woodland walk.
Recommended Varieties: Doronicum plantagineum, D. caucasicum, D. caucasicum 'Magnificum', *D.* 'Mme. Mason'.

Drooping leucothoe; see Leucothoe

Endymion hispanicus
(en-DI-mee-on his-PAN-i-cus) known also as **Scilla campanulata wood hyacinth, Spanish bluebells,** medium shade, easy, bulb.
Zones: 3 to 9
Height: 12 to 15 inches
Colors: Blue, purple, rose, white
Characteristics: This is among the latest spring bulbs to flower. It is extremely easy to grow and will live forever, forming impressive colonies. It bears graceful, delicate, bell-like blooms on sturdy, erect spikes up to 15 inches high. Blooming in late May, its clear, pastel colors are a lovely complement to the vivid color of tulips and azaleas.
Cultural Information: Performs best in rich, well-drained soils. Humus-rich soil of woodland most helpful. Plant 6 inches deep; this makes it easy to overplant it with annuals for summer. Plant 3 inches apart and set out in large clusters. Wood hyacinth has average moisture requirements. It is undemanding and lasts for years, increasing very rapidly. Leave the heavy foliage uncut after flowering.
Uses: Cutting, naturalizing, rock garden, bedding, companion plant.

Dodocatheon *species*

Doronicum caucasicum *'Magnificum'*

Endymion hispanicus

English ivy; see *Hedera*

Epimedium (ep-i-MEE-dium) **barrenwort, bishop's hat,** all types of shade, easy, perennial.

🌢

Zones: 3 to 8
Height: 9 to 15 inches
Colors: Rose, cream, purple, yellow
Characteristics: Whatever the degree of shade, *Epimedium* will grow there. It grows in the densest of shade even in virtually barren areas, and can compete with tree roots. This delicate-looking plant has tiny orchidlike flowers (shaped like a bishop's mitre) that appear in May. In spring the heart-shaped leaves, 2 to 3 inches long and tinged with red, unfold. They change to green in summer and bronze in fall. The plant is hardy and spreads to grow in clumps. It makes an excellent groundcover beneath trees, along woodland paths and in a rock garden. *Epimedium grandiflorum* is one of the largest species in a pale pink; *E. grandiflorum* 'Rose Queen' also has pink flowers with white-tipped spurs and crimson leaves; *E. grandiflorum* 'White Queen' has large white flowers.

Cultural Information: Epimedium grows best in medium to full shade with soil that is rich, acidic and moist. They will also tolerate deep shade if the drainage is good but will not produce as many flowers. Plant 10 inches apart, as they will fill in on their own without overcrowding. In early spring or fall, propagate by dividing the clumps. Cut off old leaves. Because their roots will compete successfully with other roots, you can plant them under shrubs or trees. In early spring cut plants back to the ground and remove dead growth from previous year before new foliage appears. They are rarely bothered by pests.
Uses: Groundcover, under trees and shrubs, woodland path, barren spots, rock garden.
Recommended Varieties: Epimedium grandiflorum 'Rose Queen', *E. grandiflorum* 'White Queen'.

Erythronium Dens-canis (e-rith-ROAN-ium denz Kanis) **dog-tooth violet,** medium to full shade, easy, perennial.

Zones: 3 to 9
Height: 6 to 7 inches
Colors: Yellow, pink, cream, lavender, rose

Characteristics: Most of the *Erythronium* species are known as the trout lily, but *E. Dens-canis* was one of the first to be named, and because its long, white tuberous roots resemble canine teeth, these plants were called *Dens-canis,* or dogtooth violet. "Violet" was once a general term applied to many small purple flowers. This truly wonderful plant has delicately scented nodding flowers that are lilylike in colors of yellow, pink, cream, lavender and rose. Two bright green, darkly mottled basal leaves carpet the ground. It blooms in April for one to two weeks. It does well at the base of trees (in woodland settings). It may take several years to become established. *E. Dens-canis* 'Lilac Wonder' has large lilac flowers and is one of my favorites. 'White Splendor' has the largest flowers and is pure white.
Cultural Information: Moist soil rich in humus is preferred. Set the bulbs 2 or 3 inches apart, 3 inches deep; planting the bulbs close together makes for the best effect. Plant with the thin end of the corms facing upward. Keep well watered until plant is established, not waterlogged.

Below left: Epimedium *species*

Below right: Erythronium Dens–canis *'Pagoda'*

Leave undisturbed after planting.
Use: Naturalizing.
Recommended Varieties: Erythronium Dens-canis 'Lilac Wonder', _E. Dens-canis_ 'White Splendor', _E. Dens-canis_ 'Pagoda'.

Euonymus Fortunei (yew-ON-im-us for-toon-AY-ee) **winter-creeper,** medium shade to full sun, easy, perennial. ◗

Zones: 5 to 8
Height: ½ inch to 2 feet
Colors: Flowers are inconspicuous; grown for foliage—some varieties purple, rosy red, whitish yellow
Characteristics: One of the most colorful and hardy vines and groundcovers to be had; there are other _Euonymus_ species that are shrubs. This is a trailing evergreen that can climb to 35 feet. It is grown for attractive foliage that forms a dense carpet on trailing stems that root as they move along the surface. The unusual thing about this plant is that young plants keep uniform foliage until "maturity," and then produce a different foliage in slightly different colors. _Euonymus_ leaves no room for weeds and is used widely to check erosion on banks and slopes. It is also very effective for hiding rocky ground. _E. Fortunei_ 'Colorata' is an excellent rambler with leaves that turn purple in the fall. _E._ 'Variegata' is bright green and yellow.
Cultural Information: Plant 1 to 2 feet apart in spring or fall in medium shade and well-drained soil enriched with one part peat moss or leaf mold to every two parts soil. Add a permanent mulch of wood chips, peat moss or bark 2 to 3 inches deep. To propagate, divide plants in spring or early fall or propagate from cuttings. In dense shade where the microclimate is cooler, mildew is often a problem. Scale can also be a problem, and deer do like this plant. It is drought tolerant.
Uses: Groundcover, under trees and shrubs, lawn substitute, to hide stumps.
Recommended Varieties: Euonymus Fortunei 'Colorata', _E. Fortunei_ 'Variegata'.

Fairy candles; see _Cimicifuga_

Ferns; see chart, pages 32–33.

Fetterbush; see _Leucothoe_

Fibrous begonia; see _Begonia_

Flowering tobacco; see _Nicotiana_

Foamflower; see _Tiarella_

Forget-me-not; see _Myosotis_

Forget-me-not, perennial; see _Brunnera_

Fothergilla (foth-er-GILL-a) Native American, light to medium shade, easy, shrub. 🐢

Zones: 5 to 9
Height: 3 to 9 feet
Color: White
Characteristics: A native of North Carolina and Alabama, this slow-growing shrub is related to witch hazel. Tiny white flowers in globular clusters appear on bare branches in spring and look like little shaving brushes. The flowers have no petals and consist

Euonymus Fortunei
'Variegata'

of white stamens and yellow anthers. The fragrant flowers are said to smell like honey. In fall the leaves turn orange, then crimson. _Fothergilla Gardenii_ is a choice dwarf with creamy white flowers with a honey fragrance, excellent with azaleas and rhododendron. _F. Gardenii_ 'Blue Mist' is a new variety with lovely blue flowers.
Cultural Information: Plant in cool, moist, well-drained, acid soil consisting of one part peat moss to two parts soil. Protect from wind, and in northern areas of growing zones protect roots with mulch. To propagate take cuttings from new growth in late spring or early summer, or use root cuttings taken in spring or fall.
Uses: Against a wall or fence, in front of evergreens, woodland.
Recommended Varieties: Fothergilla Gardenii 'Dwarf Fothergilla', _F. Gardenii_ 'Blue Mist', _F. major_ 'Large Fothergilla'.

Foxglove; see _Digitalis_

Funkia; see _Hosta,_ pages 28–30.

Fothergilla Gardenii

Galium odoratum

Galanthus nivalis

Galanthus nivalis (gay-LAN-thus ni-VAL-us) **snowdrop,** light to medium shade, easy, bulb. 🐢

Zones: 3 to 10
Height: 3 to 4 inches
Color: White
Characteristics: This spring-flowering bulb comes up so early it pops through late snows when in bloom. This charming, old-fashioned favorite has gracefully nodding white, fragrant flowers 1 inch long. It blooms in early March for two to three weeks. An excellent bulb for naturalizing under trees, shrubs and in the woodland garden.
Cultural Information: A very undemanding plant. Any soil is fine as long as moisture is provided. *Galanthus* can be left undisturbed for years. Because the leaves wither soon after the flowers die, this plant is nice in foreground plantings. If left alone it will usually increase by itself. Works nicely with an evergreen groundcover. Divide after flowering.
Forcing Instructions: Blooms in late winter. Emerges several weeks after planting. Use a

6-inch pot with good drainage material such as broken crockery, gravel or pebbles in the bottom. Use one part peat moss, one part Burpee Planting Formula and one part sharp sand or perlite with three to five ounces ground limestone added per bushel of mixture. Plant ½ inch deep and space 2 to 4 inches apart. Water well.
Uses: Edging, naturalizing, rock garden, forcing.

Galium odoratum (gay-LEE-um o-dor-AH-tum) **sweet woodruff,** medium shade, easy, perennial.

Zones: All
Height: 8 inches
Color: White
Characteristics: This old-time flavoring herb has the scent of fresh-cut hay. It has a thin-rooted stem with narrow whorls of evergreen leaves topped with sprays of tiny white flowers that, although small, produce an excellent display. *Galium odoratum* blooms from May to June and is a wonderful carpeting plant as it spreads very quickly. It makes a good groundcover for moist, light soil in medium shade, especially under trees (even shallow-rooted ones). It

is a nice companion plant for forget-me-nots and *Doronicum* and with shrubs and spring bulbs.
Cultural Information: Woodruff thrives in a well-drained, slightly acid, rich soil. Plant in spring or fall. The best method of propagation is to lift and separate the plants and replant the rooted pieces. Plant rooted pieces in April or May and it will cover the ground by September.
Uses: Groundcover, under trees, north wall.

Garden balsam; see *Impatiens Balsamina*

Garden spirea; see *Astilbe*

Gentian; see *Gentiana*

Gentiana (jen-she-AY-na) **gentian,** Native American, medium shade, moderate, perennial. 💧

Zones: 2 to 6
Height: 4 inches to 6 feet, depending on variety
Colors: Blue, violet
Characteristics: *Gentiana* comprises an enormous group with a wealth of beautiful flowers. Many varieties thrive in different

Gentiana asclepiadea

climates, flowering from May through October depending on the variety. *G. Andrewsii* is a North American native found in marshes and along the banks of streams from Quebec to Manitoba and south to North Carolina and Missouri. It blooms in late summer.

Cultural Information: Plant in fresh, well-drained soil approximately 6 to 12 inches apart. Propagate by sowing or dividing clumps. Plant in early fall or spring. The addition of peat and coarse sand is recommended. Disastrous rot can occur from excess moisture in winter. Surround base of plant with 1-inch layer of shredded leaves or pine needles; gravel is best kept in the rock garden. *G. septemfida* 'Crested Gentian' and *G. septemfida lagodechiana* are easier and more reliable species; *G. Andrewsii* is drought resistant and heat tolerant; *G. asclepiadea* has large blue trumpets.

Uses: Rock garden, in a border, bog garden.

Recommended: Gentiana septemfida, G. septemfida lagodechiana, G. Andrewsii, G. asclepiadea.

Geranium (jur-AY-nium) **cranesbill,** light to medium shade, easy, perennial.

Zones: 3 to 8
Height: 14 inches
Colors: Rose, lavender, pink
Characteristics: These are excellent hardy perennials, not to be confused with the "geraniums" of window-box fame, which aren't *Geranium* at all, but rather *Pelargonium.* These geraniums have maple-leaflike leaves and

produce five-petaled flowers during summer and into fall. The name cranesbill comes from the English, after the long-beaked seed head.

Geranium dalmaticum is a very popular, hardy geranium and is most attractive when planted in groups along the edge or border of a garden. It is also quite nice with rock garden plants or alliums. It comes in pink and white. *G. maculatum,* also called wild geranium, has a branching habit very pretty with ferns; its lavender-pink flowers are borne in loose clusters blooming in spring and early summer. *G.* 'Johnson's Blue' has bright blue flowers, a real winner.

Cultural Information: Cranesbill grows vigorously in any well-drained soil, and quickly establishes clumps that become so dense they're almost weedproof. Plant 10 to 14 inches apart in slightly acid, rich, moist soil. Propagate in spring or fall by taking root cuttings and setting them 1 inch deep, or from seeds sown as soon as they ripen. Seedlings will bloom in two to three years. They have no serious pest problems.

Uses: In a border, rock garden, woodland.

Recommended Varieties: Geranium maculatum, G. Endressii 'Wargrave Pink', *G. dalmaticum, G.* 'Johnson's Blue'.

Globeflower; see *Trollius*

Goatsbeard; see *Aruncus*

Goldenstar; see *Chrysogonum*

Gooseneck; see *Lysimachia*

Geranium Endressii '*Wargrave Pink*'

Hamamelis (ham-am-EE-lis) **witch hazel,** Native American, light to medium shade, easy, shrub. 🐢

Zones: 4 to 8
Height: 6 to 20 feet
Colors: White, yellow, red, orange
Characteristics: Witch hazel is known for its intensely fragrant flowers that appear during the winter on some species. Their small, bright yellow or red flowers are charming, particularly when brought inside during the middle of winter and forced into bloom. Most species have yellow fall color but *H. japonica* has red. It is not a shrub for the small garden as it can grow to 20 feet high and just as wide. Some hold their dead leaves through fall and winter, making it difficult to see the flowers.

One of the best witch hazels is a hybrid, *H. × intermedia* 'Arnold Promise', with golden yellow flowers in late winter or early spring. The fall color is a rich crimson and yellow. Chinese witch hazel (*H. mollis*) is

Hamamelis × intermedia '*Arnold Promise*'

Hedera Helix

valued for its early blooms and fragrance. The common witch hazel *(H. virginiana)* is not as ornamental as *H. mollis*.

Cultural Information: Plant in sandy loam. The native kinds usually tolerate more shade. All are pest free. Witch hazel will not tolerate drought.

Uses: Background, small tree, in front of evergreens, border for winter walks.

Recommended Varieties: Hamamelis × intermedia 'Arnold Promise', *H. japonica, H. mollis, H. virginiana*.

Hedera (HED-er-a) **ivy, English ivy,** all types of shade, easy, vine. **H. Helix English ivy;** *H. colchica* **Persian ivy;** *H. canariensis* **Algerian ivy;** all types of shade, easy, vine. 🌡 💧

Zones: 5 to 9

Height: 4 to 6 inches

Colors: Green or variegated foliage

Characteristics: The ivies are evergreen plants grown widely. They are ideal as a groundcover for barren spots or shady banks. They grow up trees and around buildings and can cover fences, stumps and posts. They spread rapidly, check erosion, adapt to almost any kind of climate and require almost no maintenance. Ivy produces a dense carpet of triangular, dark green foliage. These vines climb by attaching small, rootlike appendages to the wall or other means of support. When ivies reach their full height and can climb no farther, they produce yellow-green flowers. English ivy can climb to 50 to 100 feet; Persian

ivy, 20 to 30 feet. There are so many varieties from which to choose. The garden of the American Horticultural Society in Virginia has more than 160 varieties.

Cultural Information: Ivies are grown easily in almost any soil, but to establish plants quickly it is best to use moist, well-drained soil that is neutral or slightly acid. When starting an ivy bed, purchase well-established plants and space 12 inches apart. Keep soil moist but not soggy until established. Ivy thrives in medium shade but grows in dense shade too; growth will be slower in dense shade. Fertilize each spring with an all-purpose, slow-release fertilizer. Prune climbing ivy in early spring, cutting vines close to their support. Propagation from root cuttings can be done almost any time. Seed can be sown as soon as ripe or it can be stored in a cool place for up to a year. Watch for scale, ivy aphid, mealy bugs and oleander scale.

Uses: Groundcover, in front of a border, hanging basket.

Recommended Varieties: Hedera Helix 'Baltica', *H. Helix* 'Buttercup', *H. Helix* 'Galaxy', *H. colchica, H. canariensis*.

Helleborus (hell-e-BOR-us) **Lenten rose, Christmas rose,** light to medium shade, moderate, perennial. 🌡 ❄

Zones: 4 to 9

Height: 1 to 2 feet

Colors: Pink, rose, purple, white

Characteristics: This hardy, erect perennial belongs to the buttercup family. It is one of the first plants to bloom and announce the new season, opening with the snowdrops in February or March, and continues blooming for weeks due to the cool weather; it often lasts until May. The flowers are practically hidden by the large foliage early in the season but are easier to see later when they rise above the foliage. The cup-shaped flowers, up to 2½ inches across, hold yellow stamens and are sometimes speckled with purple. The foliage is evergreen but suffers from the ravages of winter and replaces itself in the spring. The Christmas rose *(Helleborus niger)* blooms first, with creamy green flowers that fade to brownish yellow or purplish. Later, the Lenten rose *(H. orientalis)* blooms with white or pink-tinged flowers. The Christmas rose is hardier.

Cultural Information: Helleborus

Helleborus niger

thrives best in humus-rich soil that is well drained. Add plenty of leaf mold and decayed manure. It seldom needs dividing. The plant resents transplanting and should be placed in its permanent home when young, to ease the shock. At temperatures below 15°F, bloom is delayed and unless snow protected, the evergreen leaves become scorched. Because it blooms so early, *H. niger* is best planted where it can be protected from the ravages of winter. The roots of *Helleborus* are poisonous. The plant is not difficult to grow from seed but it is slow; occasionally the plant will self-sow. Look at the base of the plant in spring for seedlings that can be moved, protected and grown in pots to be returned to a new spot in the garden the following year.

Uses: Woodland walk, in a border, shady corner.

Recommended: Helleborus niger, H. orientalis.

Hemerocallis (hem-er-o-KAL-is) daylily, sun to medium shade, easy, perennial. 🌡 💧

Zones: 3 to 10

Height: 5 feet; dwarf, 18 inches

Colors: Yellow, melon, orange, red, pink, lavender, purple

Characteristics: These wonderful flowers are perfect for one day and are gone the next. They are versatile, offer a rainbow of colors, and come in a variety of heights, forms and sizes. They multiply generously, yet do not overrun their neighbors. Daylilies are very nearly the perfect perennials. They're easy to grow, trouble-free, need little maintenance and thrive under the most unfavorable conditions.

The old-fashioned daylily, *Hemerocallis fulva,* is the one you see alongside roads across the country. It has been improved to such a degree that there is a greater profusion of blooms and they last a month or more. It is possible to plan a succession of *Hemerocallis* to bloom from June until October, depending on where you live and utilizing different cultivars. The bloom season is divided into early (late May and June), middle (late June and July) and late (August and September). The trumpet flowers are larger than ever before, some up to 9 inches across, with double, ruffled or twisted petals. They bloom over a longer period, and the color range has been expanded to include melon, pink, red, lavender and purple, in addition to the familiar yellows and oranges. There are also many attractive bicolors available now. Look for fragrant varieties like the lemon lily *(H. Lilioasphodelus).* One of the most exceptional varieties is 'Stella de Oro', a dwarf variety (18 inches), with yellow flowers that bloom continuously for three months; its compact size lends itself to being grown in a container. *H.* 'Hyperion' is a beautiful lemon yellow. 'Sweetbriar' is an old-fashioned cultivar with salmon flowers.

In addition to a profusion of bloom, daylily foliage is attractive for most, if not all, of the growing season. Its leaves emerge in pairs from an underground stem and open like fans, making handsome, fountainlike clumps. They appear in April and can hide the yellowing leaves of

Hemerocallis *'Purple Waters'*   Hemerocallis *'Goliath'*

Dwarf Hemerocallis *'Stella de Oro'*

daffodils and tulips in late spring.

Cultural Information: Daylily grows almost anywhere, but it does best in light shade in a moisture-retentive soil. Plant 2 feet apart, or closer if you're impatient for an established bed. They multiply generously but stay neat and are not invasive. If new, bare-rooted plants arrive, or if you divide plants and can't replant immediately, don't let them dry out; they will be fine in a bucket with a little water in the bottom, placed in a cool spot for a few days, if the water is changed daily. When they start to crowd, in three or four years, dig up the roots in spring or fall and divide by pushing two spading forks through the clump and pull apart. Each division should have one fan of leaves. Mulch in summer to conserve moisture. Fertilize with a slow-release 12-12-12 fertilizer lightly once each spring and repeat applications during summer and fall. Make sure they are well watered weekly early in the season, as drought retards the formation of flower buds. In light shade, the production of flowers may be less satisfactory than in full sun, but you'll enjoy the foliage all season.

Uses: Cutting, in a border, accent plant, along a bank, naturalizing.

Recommended Varieties: Hemerocallis 'Stella de Oro', *H.* 'Hyperion', *H.* 'Sweetbriar', *H.* 'Ballet Dancer', *H.* 'Hearts Alive', *H.* 'Goliath', *H.* 'Purple Waters'.

Hesperis matronalis *shown with* Cheiranthus allioni

Heuchera 'Purple Palace'

Hesperis matronalis (HES-per-is ma-tron-AL-is) **dame's rocket,** light to medium shade, easy, perennial.

Zones: 3 to 8
Height: 1 to 3 feet
Colors: White, violet
Characteristics: An old-fashioned plant that has pointed leaves and spikes of four-petaled white or violet flowers. The name *Hesperis* is from *hesperes,* "the evening," and refers to the wonderful, spicy fragrance given off only in the evening. The white variety *H. matronalis alba* is much showier for the shade and seems to glow at dusk. It blooms in late spring. A biennial, *H. violacea* reseeds itself every year.
Cultural Information: Plant in light shade or medium shade in spring or fall. It will naturalize readily. It will perform better if kept moist and will benefit from a mulch. Cut stems down in autumn. This plant requires no special culture and may be propagated from seed. Plants are not readily found at nurseries but seed can usually be found in catalogs.
Uses: In a border, bank of a pool or stream.
Recommended: Hesperis matronalis, H. matronalis alba.

Heuchera (hew-KER-a) **coralbells,** Native American, medium shade, easy, perennial.

Zones: 3 to 9
Height: 1 to 2 feet
Colors: White, pink, red
Characteristics: A superb plant with semievergreen, ruffle-shaped foliage. The common name aptly describes the flower color and shape. One of this plant's best features is its ability to do well almost anywhere. The plant matures in about one year with attractively shaped leaves and long, wandlike stems that carry tiny bell flowers in early summer—and sometimes off and on again throughout the summer. The bright green or deep bronze foliage forms attractive basal clumps. Flower arrangers find its long-lasting blooms good for cutting and excellent subjects for drying. Coralbells are native to New Mexico, Arizona, and south into Mexico. *H. americana* 'Dale's Selection' is a striking native particularly at home on dry banks and tolerant of even infertile soils. Handsomely scalloped, purple-blue leaves with deep blue veins provide all-season display, enhanced in June and July by delicate sprays of white flowers tinged with green. *H. sanguinea* 'Bressingham Hybrids' has green foliage and flowers in shades of pink, white or deep rose. *H.* × 'Purple Palace' is one of the best introductions in recent years. It has deep purple foliage that turns purple-bronze in fall.
Cultural Information: Plant coralbells in spring in well-drained soil with ample humus. Set crowns 1 inch below the soil level. In spring, remove any damaged leaves to prevent them from rotting on the plant and spreading disease. As flowers fade, remove them to encourage later bloom. In severely cold areas it will be necessary to apply a mulch to ensure survival during winter. Salt hay, or any light material that doesn't pack down, should prove satisfactory as a mulch. Divide plants

in spring when they become overcrowded, usually after four to five years of flowering. New plants are easy to start from leaf cuttings made in late fall. Each cutting needs a short section of leaf stalk, in addition to an entire leaf, to root in sand. Sow seeds outdoors in spring and they will produce flowers the following year. Do not cover seeds after pressing into soil, as they need light to germinate. Sow seeds indoors in late winter or early spring at 50° to 60°F. Seeds germinate in about 20 days. There must be perfect drainage to avoid crown rot, especially in winter. Stems also may rot in heavy wet soils and humid climates. If foliage rots in summer after heavy rains, cut it away to prevent the spread of disease.

Uses: Cutting, drying, front of a border, groundcover.

Recommended Varieties: Heuchera × 'Palace Purple', *H. americana* 'Dale's Selection', *H. sanguinea* 'Bressingham Hybrids'.

Hibiscus syriacus (hy-BISK-us see-ree-AH-kus) **rose of Sharon,** medium to full shade, easy, shrub.

Zones: 5 to 9

Height: Up to 15 feet

Colors: White, rose, black-purple

Characteristics: This is an old-fashioned, deciduous shrub that thrives in the shade, needs very little attention and has lovely, late-season bloom. Most of the numerous varieties are very neat and compact, growing from 5 to 12 feet in height. They bloom in late summer when most other shrubs are out of flower. Blooms come in single, double and semidouble flowers. Double-flowered varieties don't have fruits; semidouble varieties may have only a few, if any. It is a fine seashore plant as it tolerates salt air. *H. syriacus* prefers northern climates. As self-sowing can be a problem, look for sterile varieties. *H. syriacus* 'Diana' is a white-flowered variety that doesn't self-sow. *H. syriacus* 'Southern Belle' is a pink-rose color.

Cultural Information: The double-flowered varieties root easily from cuttings of the dormant wood in early spring or from green wood in summer. Cuttings from the ripened wood should be made in the fall and heeled in out of the reach of frost in moderately dry sand. They may be put in rows in the open as soon as weather permits. The single varieties come true from seed. Young plants are susceptible to winter injury in the North, particularly their first winter, and should be well protected. Established plants usually need no protection. This plant needs little maintenance beyond an occasional thinning of branches. If you cut back the previous year's growth in spring, the flowers will be much larger.

Uses: In a border, accent plant, hedge.

Recommended Varieties: Hibiscus syriacus 'Diana', *H. syriacus* 'Southern Belle', H. 'Lord Baltimore'.

Honeysuckle; see *Lonicera*

Hosta; see pages 28–30

Hibiscus *'Lord Baltimore'*

Hibiscus syriacus *'Southern Belle'*

Hydrangea 'French Blue'

Hydrangea anomala petiolaris

Hyacinth, wood; see ***Endymion***

Hybrid anemone; see ***Anemone***

Hydrangea (hy-DRAN-jia) dense shade to full sun, easy, shrub. **Hydrangea anomala petiolaris,** dense shade to full sun, easy, vine.
Zones: 5 to 10
Height: 3 to 8 feet, by variety
Colors: Blue, white, pink
Characteristics: Hydrangea may be one of the best as well as the loveliest of plants for the shade. The flowers are very handsome when in bloom, changing in color as the flowers mature from greenish white to a deep rose. These starlike clusters also bloom in deep shades of blue and violet. It has coarse, shiny leaves 4 to 8 inches long that look attractive all season. It blooms throughout the summer and keeps a lustrous foliage in mild winter areas. It will grow in the sun but prefers shady locations and will bloom even in dense shade.

H. macrophylla, the big-leafed hydrangea, has broad, thick, shining leaves and round flower clusters that bloom throughout the summer; *H. macrophylla* 'French Blue' is a beautiful azure in large, round clusters. *H. arborescens* 'Grandiflora' has been an old favorite for more than 50 years; it was originally found near Yellow Springs, Ohio, around 1900. 'Annabelle', an *H. arborescens* 'Grandiflora' variety, bears 10-inch, round clusters of pure white flowers nearly the entire summer. *H. quercifolia*, the oak-leafed hydrangea, has a coarse, interesting texture and is a native of the southeastern United States. It can be grown in hotter, drier climates than others; it dies in the winter in the North. *H. quercifolia* 'Snowflake' has conical heads of creamy white flowers that acquire a rosy tint as they mature in autumn. *H. anomala petiolaris* is a truly spectacular vine that is most effective when climbing a shaded wall, a tree trunk or an arbor. Its white, lacy flower clusters bloom in June and stand out against a darker background. The leaves are shiny and dark green. This climbing hydrangea will spread 3 to 4 feet wide when planted on a trellis or wall, but will be bushy and compact when planted in the open. When climbing, it attaches itself to its support by means of roots along the stems, needing no additional support. It is one of the best ornamental vines available.
Cultural Information: When planted in medium shade, hydrangea flowers last longer and hold their color better. Plant in well-drained, moist, rich soil high in organic matter. *H. macrophylla* will produce blue flowers in acid soil and pink flowers in alkaline soil. To acidify the soil for blue flowers on big-leafed hydrangeas, work 1 to 2 pounds of aluminum sulfate into the soil; to acidify after planting, mix the same amount of aluminum sulfate with 7 gallons of water and apply around the plant in late winter or spring. If pruning is necessary, it should be done after flowering. If there is a cold winter and the plant dies back, it will not flower that season. The climbing hydrangea is a bit slow to get started, but once established, it makes excellent growth every year. Plant it in moist, well-drained soil enriched with compost in fall or early spring. To grow on a tree, dig a hole 3 × 3 feet about 1 foot away from the tree and set the hydrangea into it. Surround the stem with a metal or plastic collar, about 6 inches from the stem, to keep the tree roots from disturbing it. Water and never allow it to dry out, even when it's dormant. Each spring add compost to the base of the plant. To contain growth and weed out thin or dead branches, cut back after flowering. Propagate by fastening a cutting to the ground in late spring.
Uses: In a border, shady walk, accent plant. Use climbing hydrangea on trellis, tree, or shaded wall.
Recommended Varieties: Hydrangea arborescens 'Annabelle', *H. macrophylla* 'French Blue', *H. macrophylla* 'All Summer Beauty', *H. quercifolia* 'Snowflake', *H. quercifolia* 'Snow Queen', *H. anomala petiolaris*.

Hypericum (hy-PER-ik-um) **St.-John's-wort, Aaron's-beard,** Native American, medium shade, easy, shrub.

Zones: 5 to 9

Height: 4 to 6 feet; 12 to 18 inches for the dwarf shrub

Color: Yellow

Characteristics: Hypericum, unfortunately, is not used very often. This shrub has bright, open, yellow flowers with tufts of golden threads at their center, blooming on arching stems June through September. It is usually evergreen in the South. Most are vigorous and hardy. *Hypericum calycinum* is one of the best and most useful of the dwarf evergreen shrubs. It forms dense clumps of growth, not more than a foot high, with very large, bright yellow flowers. *H. patulum* 'Hidcote' has an abundance of golden yellow flowers all summer.

Hypericum is useful to brighten up rockeries, line walks and enhance perennial borders. Planted in front of spring-blooming shrubs, it adds summer color and acts as a groundcover. An attractive combination in the border is the yellow of *Hypericum* with the blue of *Aster ×Frikartii,* an equally long bloomer.

Cultural Information: Plant dwarf varieties 8 inches apart, others at least inches apart, in fall or spring in light, well-drained soil enriched with compost. Water well the first summer and watch clumps spread. They are easily divided in spring or fall. They can also be propagated by cuttings started in summer.

Uses: Rock garden, edging, in a border, groundcover.

Recommended Varieties: Hypericum calycinum, H. patulum 'Hidcote'.

Impatiens Wallerana (im-PAY-shiens wo-la-RAH-na) **busy lizzy, patient plant,** light, medium, full shade; *I. Balsamina* (bal-SAM-ee-na) **garden balsam, touch-me-not,** medium shade; *I. Schlechteri* (SHLEK-ter-i) light shade to sun, all easy bedding plants; I. Wallerana and I. Schlechteri hybrids slightly challenging to grow from seed, annual.❀

Height: 6 to 24 inches

Colors: All colors plus bicolors

Characteristics: Impatiens is indispensable for the shade garden. It grows in every type of shade except the deepest, comes in a multitude of colors, requires minimum care and is a prolific bloomer. No wonder it is so popular. The name *Impatiens* derives from a typical characteristic feature of the genus. When the seed capsules are ripe and lightly touched, they burst open with considerable force in a somewhat impatient manner; the other common name for them is touch-me-not.

I. Wallerana is unbeatable for brilliant summer-to-fall bloom in shady beds, borders and containers. The hybrid varieties have longer bloom, a wider array of colors, more uniform sizes and a few have variegated foliage. They have many improvements from the original *I. Wallerana* that came from

Right: Impatiens Wallerana 'Accent Rose Star Hybrid'
Far right: Impatiens Wallerana 'Minette Mixed'

Hypericum patulum 'Hidcote'

Impatiens wallerana 'Rosette Hybrid'

New Guinea Impatiens

Tanzania and were tender perennials. The 'Rosette' hybrid has flowers that are double and semidouble and look like miniature roses. It usually comes in a mix that includes full doubles, semidoubles and some singles, in brilliant red, scarlet, rose, pink, orange, salmon, white and red and white bicolors. 'Blitz' hybrids come in a wide variety of colors and are larger-flowered (2 inches across) on compact plants 14 to 16 inches high. 'Super Elfin' hybrids are dwarf, uniform, low, spreading plants 10 to 12 inches. The Dazzler hybrids have the widest array of colors, with 1¾-inch flowers, and are only 8 inches high.

I. Balsamina is a very easy, old-fashioned annual with double or single flowers, the former often called the rose-flowered or camellia-flowered impatiens. The plants can be from 10 inches to 3 feet tall. It self-sows readily, although the young seedlings are easy to remove from unwanted places.

I. Schlechteri, New Guinea hybrid impatiens, prefer sun but in all other ways resemble their cousins in their long bloom, bushy appearance, easy care and wide range of colors. In addition there are varieties available with dark burgundy or variegated foliage that complement and enhance their flowers.
Cultural Information: All like a rich, well-drained soil with plenty of moisture during dry periods. *I. Wallerana* will even tolerate full sun if given plenty of water. Use slow-release fertilizers, low in nitrogen, to provide nutrients during the whole growing season. Reseeds readily in

southern zones. Sow indoors anytime for houseplants.

All are easy to propagate from cuttings. If growing from seed, remember that impatiens need a minimum temperature of 70°F to germinate. New Guinea impatiens is usually propagated by cuttings. 'Tango', an AAS winner with big, bold, orange flowers 2 or more inches across, is a good variety to grow from seed. Space all types 8 to 12 inches apart.
Uses: Edging, in a border, groundcover, container plant, hanging basket.
Recommended Varieties: Rosette Hybrids, *Impatiens Balsamina*, *I.* New Guinea 'Tango', *I.* New Guinea 'Tangelow', *I.* New Guinea 'Spectra Mix', *I. Wallerana*.

Ivy; see ***Hedera***

Japanese anemone; see ***Anemone***

Japanese Solomon's seal; see ***Polygonatum***

Japanese spurge; see ***Pachysandra***

Jonquil; see ***Narcissus***

Kalmia latifolia (KAL-mee-a la-ti-FOL-ee-yah) **mountain laurel,** Native American, medium, full to dense shade, easy, shrub.
Zones: 4 to 9
Height: 15 feet or taller
Colors: White, pink, rose-red, red with white
Characteristics: The mountain laurel is a native evergreen

shrub growing from Maine southward. In the northern states it is a bush, 4 to 8 feet. Farther south it is frequently met at 20 feet. Beautiful, cup-shaped flowers varying in color from white to shades of pink bloom in mid-June. The interesting buds form flowers in loose clusters 4 to 6 inches across. The inside petals have brown dots. They are slow growing and, in youth, rounded, dense and neat. They become more open as they grow older. Prune to keep the shrub's shape—it will grow into a small tree if never pruned. *K. latifolia* 'Bullseye' is a striking red and white variety, whereas *K. latifolia* 'Sarah' is a soft red.

Breeders in Connecticut, Massachusetts and Washington have developed a number of new cultivars over the last few years with a much wider range of colors than have been available in the past. 'Pink Sunrise' and 'Pink Charm' are both beautiful shades of rosy pink. There are also new dwarf *K. myrtifolia* varieties available that grow to only 3 feet.
Cultural Information: Plant in cool, moist, well-drained soil high in organic matter. Mulch to retain moisture. To create more abundant flowering, remove mulch in spring and fertilize around base, then replace mulch. Use an organic fertilizer of cottonseed meal, bone meal and green sand in equal amounts. Use commercial 6-4-4 fertilizer mixture. To further flower production for the next year, pinch off the seed capsules when the flowers fade. Prune immediately after flowering stops. Winter damage from drying out can produce brown

Kalmia latifolia

leaf tips. There is only one serious pest: the black vine weevil. Watch for the telltale sign of nibbled leaf margins.

Uses: Companion plant, woodland, back of a border, foundation, hedge.

Recommended Varieties: Kalmia latifolia 'Pink Sunrise', *K. latifolia* 'Pink Charm', *K. latifolia* 'Bullseye', *K. latifolia* 'Sarah'.

Lady's-mantle; see ***Alchemilla***

Leadwort; see ***Ceratostigma***

Lenten rose; see ***Helleborus***

Leopard's bane; see ***Doronicum***

Lamium maculatum (LAY-mee-um ma-cu-LAY-tum) **dead nettle,** medium to full shade, easy, perennial.

Zones: 4 to 9
Height: 6 to 8 inches
Colors: White, pink
Characteristics: Here's a perfect groundcover that will brighten those dark shaded areas. Few groundcovers have as many fine qualities as dead nettle does. With small, crinkled leaves that are dark green splotched with silvery white, it makes an excellent uniform carpet in the shade. For a more interesting arrangement mix with other shade-loving plants such as hosta or ferns, combinations that produce some very effective patterns and textures. 'Beacon Silver' is a real beauty, with silver foliage edged in green. Spikes of pink flower clusters appear in April and continue into September. 'White Nancy' is also showy but

with less assertive, silvery green leaves and white flowers. *Lamium* is easy to grow, trouble-free and spreads rapidly, making it a good choice for a shady groundcover.

Cultural Information: Grows easily in medium and full shade, and although it prefers soils that are evenly moist, it will withstand drought. Any ordinary soil will do but it prefers humus and some peat occasionally. Cover the soil with a mulch to control weeds until the dead nettles have provided full cover. It is easily propagated by division in spring, or take cuttings in summer. No significant pest problems.

Uses: Groundcover, wild garden.
Recommended Varieties: Lamium maculatum 'Beacon Silver', *L. maculatum* 'White Nancy'.

Leucothoe Fontanesiana (lew-KO-tho-ee fon-tan-EE-si-ana) **drooping leucothoe, fetterbush,** Native American, medium, full dense shade, easy, shrub.

Zones: 5 to 9
Height: 3 to 5 feet
Color: White
Characteristics: An excellent small shrub, evergreen in the South and semievergreen in the North, with arching branches and sprays of white flowers on small racemes that hang down under the branches. It has dark, lustrous leaves that change colors with the season. The leaves can be up to 7 inches long and are bronze-green when young; when mature, deep green in summer and a handsome bronze in fall (sometimes lasting all winter). Because of its graceful habit it makes a terrific companion to

rhododendron, azalea and mountain laurel. Use leucothoe on shaded slopes or in woodland settings.

Cultural Information: Plant 4 feet apart in acid, moist, well-drained soil high in organic matter. Protect from drought and drying winds. Watch for leaf spot. Pruning is rarely necessary but should be done directly after flowering. The older stems should be removed to keep the shrub vigorous. Pruning older plants to the ground will rejuvenate them. Leucothoe looks best when kept under 3 feet tall. Propagate from stem cuttings of new growth taken in late summer or early fall and place in moist soil and peat moss until roots develop. During first year protect with leaf mulch or wood chips.

Uses: Massing, in a border, naturalizing, woodland, shady slopes.
Recommended Varieties: Leucothoe 'Girard's Rainbow', *L.* 'Nana' (variegated).

Lily; see page 17

Lily of the valley; see ***Convallaria***

Lilyturf; see ***Liriope***

Liriope Muscari (li-ri-O-pe mus-KAR-ee) **lilyturf,** light to medium shade, easy, perennial.

🖤 💧
Zones: 6 to 10
Height: 1 to 1½ feet
Colors: White, violet, mauve, lavender
Characteristics: Liriope looks like a large grape hyacinth that flowers at the end of summer. The plain or striped foliage of graceful, curving, grasslike leaves with leathery texture is just as decorative as the flowers. It is

Lamium maculatum
'Beacon Silver'

Leucothoe Fontanesiana 'Rainbow'

Liriope Muscari
'Big Blue'

Lobelia Cardinalis

evergreen in the South but the ravages of a northern winter require shearing damaged foliage in the spring or fall. The blue-black berries that follow the flowers can be picked for late fall arrangements. *Liriope* does well under a wide range of light conditions and is a good groundcover for under a tree, or decorative edging to a walk.

L. Muscari 'Big Blue' has deep green foliage and reaches 15 inches. *L. Muscari* 'Variegata' grows 18 inches tall and has green leaves variegated in yellow.

Cultural Information: If you can provide for good drainage, *Liriope* will grow in almost any soil. A neutral to slightly acid soil is preferable. It requires ample moisture but can withstand short periods of drought. In cold areas, leaves may brown in late winter and should be cut back in spring and added to the compost pile. Divide tufted or rhizomatous plants in early spring before new growth begins. It can, however, remain undisturbed indefinitely. Self-sown seedlings may be inferior.

Uses: Cutting, in a border, groundcover, edging, under trees.

Recommended Varieties: Liriope Muscari 'Big Blue', *L. Muscari* 'Variegata'.

Lobelia Erinus
'String of Pearls, Mixed'

Lobelia (lo-BEE-lia) **cardinal flower, blue cardinal flower,** Native American, medium to full shade, moderate, perennial. 🌡

Zones: 2 to 8

Height: 2 to 4 feet

Colors: Red, blue

Characteristics: L. Cardinalis has dazzling scarlet flowers in late summer and early fall. This stately plant grows 2 to 4 feet and is splendid for growing next to watersides and wild gardens where soil is moist. The individual flowers are small but many and grow in a spike along the upper 6 to 8 inches of the stem. They are attractive to hummingbirds. The leaves are dark green and of an oblong shape. They form opposite to each other in whorls along the stalk. The stalk grows 2 to 4 feet and is topped with the brilliant flowers. It can be short-lived but will self-sow where happy. *L. siphilitica* has blue flowers on bushier plants and is not as fussy as its brighter relative, growing quite happily in drier shady spots.

Cultural Information: Best grown in well-drained, sandy loam that is high in organic matter and kept evenly moist. Keep well watered and remove faded flower stalks to help the plant produce more, although smaller, flower spikes. Mulch in summer to retain moisture and again in winter to protect the crowns. Divide by lifting the clump and remove and reset the outside clusters of new basal growth in early fall. If divided yearly it will live longer. It can be grown from seeds sown in the fall to bloom the following summer.

Uses: Moist shady spot, natural garden, woodland, bank of stream.

Recommended: Lobelia Cardinalis, L. siphilitica.

Lobelia Erinus (lo-BEE-lia e-RY-nus), light shade, easy, annual. ✿

Height: 4 to 6 inches (dwarf varieties), 4 inches (trailing varieties)

Colors: White, rose, blue, violet, some with white eyes

Characteristics: The original *Lobelia Erinus* was introduced in 1752 from the Cape of Good Hope and ever since gardeners have showcased them in their gardens. These dark blue flowering plants are compact, growing to only 6 inches high with small dainty flowers and green-to-bronze leaves. Some new varieties are wonderful draping over the edges and down the sides of containers and window boxes. *L. Erinus* 'Sapphire' is a trailing variety that is charming with its dark blue flowers accented by a white eye. The dwarf varieties make good edgers, and all varieties are suited to planting in a rock garden. 'Blue Moon' is a delicate edging for a bed of white impatiens and an excellent choice for southern gardens where it stands up well to prolonged high temperatures.

Cultural Information: Lobelia thrives in ordinary garden soil. Plant in light shade. Cut back growth to 2 inches after first blooms start to fade, to help it continue flowering. It is short-lived but often self-sows. It may stop flowering if summers are too hot, and doesn't thrive where temperatures and humidity are high. When starting indoors, keep seedlings evenly moist until the plants are established. The seed is very fine and should not be covered as it needs light to germinate and is slow growing as a seedling. Can be propagated in the fall from cuttings for indoor winter bloom on a sunny window. The plants are poisonous if eaten. Space plants 6 inches apart.

Uses: Container plant, edging, front of a border, hanging basket.

Recommended Varieties: Lobelia Erinus 'Blue Moon', *L. Erinus* 'Sapphire', *L. Erinus* 'String of Pearls, Mixed'.

Lobularia maritima (lob-yew-LAY-ria ma-RI-ti-ma) **sweet alyssum,** light shade, easy, annual. ❀ 🐝.

Height: 3 to 4 inches

Colors: White, pink, blue, violet, deep rose,

Characteristics: An invaluable summer bedding annual, alyssum is a spreading, mat-forming annual with tiny, delicate flowers that are wonderfully fragrant. It blooms from late spring to frost and has narrow, hairy leaves. Mature alyssum spreads several times its height. A wonderful plant for edging or the rock garden. It grows well in the crevices of stone paths or stone walls. Dwarf varieties like 'Little Gem' and 'Snow Queen' are perfect edging plants for beds and borders. 'Lilac Queen' and 'Violet Queen' are lavender-rose varieties.

Cultural Information: This plant is quick to germinate and early to flower. Can be directly sown outdoors where it is to grow after all danger of heavy frost; there is no real advantage to starting seeds indoors. Simply scatter seeds on a prepared bed and don't cover them. The plant will frequently reseed itself.

When it starts to slow its bloom, cut off flowers and it will bloom all summer. Most books tell you to shear the tops but that gives the plant a shaved, unnatural look that takes several weeks to outgrow. If you have a small area, use scissors and give a more natural, less even cut. Fertilize and it will grow back sooner and continue to flower until heavy frost. Space plants 6 inches apart.

Uses: Edging, container plant, houseplant, groundcover, front of a border, window box, rock garden, strawberry jar.

Recommended Varieties: Lobularia maritima, L. maritima 'Little Gem', 'Snow Queen', 'Lilac Queen', 'Color Carpet'.

Lonicera (lon-IS-er-a) **honeysuckle,** light to medium shade, easy, vine. 🐝.

Zones: 5 to 9

Height: 30 feet

Colors: Yellow, coral, red, white

Characteristics: Lonicera is the common honeysuckle vine. It is hardy; many varieties are invasive and most have fragrant flowers. The blossoms open at evening, are creamy white and especially fragrant, the better to attract night-flying moths. After fertilization, the corollas turn pale yellow. Honeysuckle needs wire netting or a lattice to twine about, but is not fussy. It thrives even at the seashore and blooms, off and on, all summer. The common yellow and white, very fragrant honeysuckle, *L. japonica* and *L. japonica* 'Halliana'

Lobularia maritima *'Color Carpet'*

(Hall's honeysuckle), run rampant when given perfect conditions, especially in the South where the plant isn't stopped by freezing winter. However, it is excellent for checking erosion on a steep hill. It is a better vine for northern gardens where it is not invasive and won't climb trees, shade them from the sun and kill them as *L. japonica* 'Halliana' can. Other varieties like *L. Heckrottii* are everblooming with bright coral and yellow flowers. Both buds and blooms are present at the same time, giving a lovely two-toned effect. It is showier, well-behaved everywhere, and attracts hummingbirds, but lacks the wonderful fragrance.

Cultural Information: Honeysuckle makes very few demands on the gardener. It flourishes in ordinary soils, even poor or heavy soils. It will need to be pruned back to encourage branching or to keep it to a particular size. It is best to prune in the fall right after it stops flowering, or in the early spring in the North before it leafs-out. Propagation by seeds or cuttings.

Recommended Varieties: Lonicera japonica 'Halliana', *L. Heckrottii.*

Lonicera Heckrottii

Loosestrife; see *Lysimachia*

Lungwort; see *Pulmonaria*

Lysimachia (ly-sim-AK-ia) **loosestrife, gooseneck,** light shade to sun, easy, perennial.

Zones: 4 to 9
Height: 2½ to 3 feet
Colors: White, yellow
Characteristics: Lysimachia belongs to the *Primula* family and is a showy garden plant, easy to grow, and is useful where it can run wild without overrunning less vigorous plants. Blooms early to late summer depending on variety.

Lysinachia clethroides has graceful, curving white spikes, resembling a goose neck, hence the common name, and blooms in midsummer. Growth is vigorous in the north but not difficult to control. In southern areas, it is extremely invasive and when taking out, be careful not to leave any piece of root, for any little root left is capable of forming a new plant.

Creeping Jenny *(L. Nummularia)* is shallow rooted and spreading, but not a troublemaker. It

Lysimachia clethroides

Lysimachia Nummularia

has a trailing, creeping habit with large, showy yellow flowers and blooms all summer. 'Aurea' is a cultivar with yellowish leaves but insignificant flowers. *L. punctata* is a tall, spiky plant covered with yellow flowers in midsummer that likes moist, shady places and has naturalized along country roads, earning it the name of "ditch witch."

Cultural Information: All garden varieties are best if planted in moist, rich soil, but average soil is satisfactory if it retains moisture. Otherwise, add peat moss or compost and water during dry spells. Taller varieties may need supports. Plants can be divided in the spring. Sow seeds in early spring. Grow *L. clethroides* in a container (provide good drainage) sunk in the soil, to prevent the roots from spreading.

Uses: In a border, cutting, wildflower garden, woodland walk, groundcover.

Recommended: Lysimachia clethroides, L. Nummularia.

Mahonia aquifolium (ma-HO-nia ak-wil-fol-EE-um) **Oregon holly grape,** Native American, light to medium shade, easy, shrub.

Zones: 5 to 8
Height: 3 to 5 feet
Colors: Yellow flowers in spring, blue-black berries in summer
Characteristics: A superb evergreen shrub that is among the most adaptable and useful plants for the shade garden. It thrives in any shade, but performs best in medium to light shade. The Oregon holly grape is a member of the barberry family. It has large, hollylike leaves, and

Mahonia aquifolium

charming yellow flowers form clusters at the tips of branches in late spring and early summer. After the flowers will follow clusters of blue-black berries that taste something like currants.

Cultural Information: Plant in well-drained, moist, acid soil 2 feet apart and it will form a thick groundcover and effective border. It will thrive anywhere except in full sun in the hottest climates. It is drought resistant. Prune to maintain desired height in early spring. It looks best kept at about 3 feet, and tends to flop over if much taller. Propagate by removing and replanting suckers. In northern zones protect from winter winds. Mulch with 2 to 3 inches of well-rotted oak leaves or pine needles to prevent loss of moisture. Fertilize in early spring around base of plant. Watch for barberry loper.

Uses: Foundation, groundcover, border, rock garden, woodland, barrier plant.

Megasea; see *Bergenia*

Mertensia virginica

(MER-ten-sia vir-GIN-i-ka) **Virginia bluebells,** Native American, light to dense shade, easy, perennial.

Zones: 3 to 8
Height: 1 to 2 feet
Colors: Sky blue with pink or purple tints, white
Characteristics: One of the loveliest wildflowers to appear in spring, Virginia bluebells has bell-shaped flowers that droop in one-sided clusters that hang gracefully at the end of the stems. The plant blooms in April and May and the foliage dies back and totally disappears in July, so a label indicating its location is useful. Because it goes dormant early, try planting it with clump-forming ferns and hostas. It also looks striking with trilliums. This native can be found from New York to Alabama, and west to the Great Plains.
Cultural Information: This blue beauty likes shade and moisture. Plant the crowns 1 inch below the soil and 8 inches apart in dense shade in cool, moist soil high in organic matter. Allow foliage to die naturally. Sow seeds in spring, summer or fall and seedlings will flower in 3 years. Bees love Virginia bluebells.
Uses: Wildflower garden, woodland path, rock garden, in a border, naturalizing.
Recommended Varieties: Mertensia virginica 'Alba', *M. virginica* 'Rubra'.

Monkshood; see *Aconitum*

Mother-in-law plant; see *Caladium*

Mountain laurel; see *Kalmia*

Myosotis (mi-o-SO-tis) **forget-me-not,** light to full shade, easy, perennial, biennial, annual. 🌡

Zones: 3 to 8
Height: 7 to 12 inches
Colors: Bright blue, pink and white
Characteristics: Forget-me-not is one of the most special flowers of spring. Its popularity is due to its profusion of blooms and because it is easy to grow. It can be an annual, biennial or perennial. All varieties are low-growing and hardy. *M. sylvatica* is a very popular annual and biennial, and one of the truest blues of the flower kingdom. It's lovely naturalized in woodlands, or under shrubs where it reseeds itself. Plant seeds in the fall over tulips and come spring you'll have tulips blooming in a sea of blue forget-me-nots. *M. scorpioides* is the old-fashioned perennial variety that grows only 8 inches tall (prostrate), bearing curling stems laden with soft blue flowers, each with a cheery yellow eye. *M. scorpioides semperflorens* is a dwarf variety. All make enchanting spring bouquets.
Cultural Information: This is a good plant for moist conditions. This means additional water will be required during periods of prolonged hot, dry weather. Seeds need darkness for germination. *Myosotis* stays in bloom longer if not allowed to go to seed. Seed can be sown in fall, started early indoors or direct-sown outdoors early in spring. Space individual plants 6 inches apart.
Uses: edging, bedding, cutting, groundcover, rock garden, hanging basket, companion plant.

Recommended: Myosotis sylvatica 'Blue Bird', *M. scorpioides, M. scorpioides semperflorens.*

Myrtle, creeping; see *Vinca*

Narcissus (nar-SIS-us) **daffodil, jonquil,** light to medium shade, easy, bulb. 🐞

Zones: 4 to 10
Height: 6 to 20 inches
Colors: Yellow, white, cream, pink, orange, and bicolors
Characteristics: The name daffodil is commonly applied to all *Narcissus* with large trumpet flowers. The terms *daffodil, jonquil,* and *narcissus* are used interchangeably but, as a common name, jonquil should be used only to refer to a smaller number of particular species.

Daffodils come in a wide range of colors and selections. When purchasing your plants, choose both early and late varieties in order to prolong the

Mertensia virginica

Myosotis sylvatica
'Blue Bird'

Narcissus 'King Alfred'

Above left: Narcissus *'Ice Follies'*

Above right: Narcissus *'Cheerfulness' and 'Yellow Cheerfulness'*

Nicotiana alata *'Nicki Hybrid Mixed'*

bloom from early spring to May. The choices of varieties are endless. There are trumpet, large-cupped, double, small, large—something for everyone. When choosing it really comes down to your personal taste. Blooming begins in February with 'February Gold'. Most varieties bloom in March and April, lasting about 3 weeks. Some varieties are more hardy than others, and don't require dividing as often, among them species or miniature types. 'Standard Valve' is excellent for the South, 'Ceylon' is long lasting and 'Cheerfulness' is an enchanting double.

Cultural Information: Light, well-drained soil, rich in humus, is best. Work soil a few inches deeper than is necessary to plant, about 3 times as deep as the bulb is long. These are great feeders and rapid growers, quickly crowding each other and exhausting soil nutrients. When crowded they must be separated or they cease to bloom. Fertilizer should not touch bulbs. They require normal moisture, but some tolerate wet soil conditions better than others. The best time for planting is late August or early September, later in the north. Remove all faded flowers. Divide when plants produce nothing but foliage. Dig after foliage dies down. Because they are poisonous, the bulbs are rarely bothered by animals.

Uses: Edging, cutting, naturalizing, rock garden, bedding, forcing, potted plant, companion plant.

Recommended Varieties: Narcissus 'Dutch Master', *N.* 'Standard Value', *N.* 'Mount Hood', *N.* 'Ice Follies', *N.* 'Red Hill', *N.* 'Cheerfulness', *N.* 'Ceylon', *N.* 'King Alfred'.

Nicotiana (ni-ko-shee-AY-na)

flowering tobacco, Native American from Brazil, medium shade to sun, moderately easy, annual.

Height: 16 inches to 4 feet, depending variety

Colors: White, pink, rose, red, purple, burgundy

Characteristics: For the middle or back of a border, *Nicotiana* is unbeatable. The light green leaves are broad and make a handsome display in sun or medium shade, and the starlike, trumpet flowers are profuse. *Nicotiana sylvestris* was a great favorite years ago for its wonderful fragrance, which is strongest at night, but it fell from favor because it needed to be staked. Dwarf versions of *Nicotiana alata*, the Nicki Hybrid, are better behaved. They don't need staking, have wonderful color, and long bloom (but little fragrance). Flowering tobacco is perennial in Zone 10. The newer hybrids stay open during the day while the old-fashioned, open-pollinated varieties close in cloudy weather.

Nicki Hybrids are free-flowering, versatile, semidwarf (16 to 18 inches) varieties, with the old-fashioned star-shaped, tubular flowers that bloom all season in a wide veriety of colors.

Cultural Information: Nicotiana grows easily from seed, but because seed is very fine a garden blanket will be helpful to keep seeds from washing away in heavy rains. Don't cover the seeds with soil, as they need light to germinate. Unless growing under lights, don't sow before March 1, as they need long days to bloom. *Nicotiana* prefers a good garden soil with lots of organic matter. Additional moisture may be needed during periods of prolonged hot, dry weather. Thrives in humid areas but suffers in the prolonged hot, humid conditions of southern gardens, where it is best grown

as a spring/early summer flower, discarded when it starts to look ragged. Space 9 inches apart for dwarf varieties, up to 2 feet for taller varieties.
Uses: In a border, containers, plant, cutting.
Recommended Varieties: Nicotiana sylvestris, Nicki Hybrids, Domino series.

Oregon holly grape; see *Mahonia*

Pachysandra (pak-is-AND-ra) **Japanese spurge,** medium to dense shade, easy, perennial. ♦
Zones: 4 to 8
Height: 6 to 12 inches
Color: White
Characteristics: Pachysandra is the most popular groundcover in the United States, because it is hardy, fast growing, long lived, attractively flowered and spreads quickly by underground runners. The leaves are 2 to 4 inches long, wedge-shaped and toothed at the tips. It grows in clusters and creates a bushy carpet of foliage that stays green even throughout the winter. In spring, tiny white flowers bloom short and spiky. The flowers are sometimes followed by tiny white berries in the fall.
Cultural Information: Plant in moist, rich, acid soil, preferably in medium shade. In dense shade areas add peat moss. Plant 6 to 12 inches apart in spring or early summer and water regularly until established. Give a complete fertilizer feeding in the spring. Plant where it won't harm other plants; it is invasive enough to take moisture and nutrients from other plants. It spreads quickly by branching root stocks. When

given too much sun it turns yellow. Propagate by lifting and cutting runners that contain several new plants, or from rooted stem cuttings that are taken in early summer. Watch for leaf blight.
Uses: Groundcover, under trees.
Recommended Varieties: Pachysandra terminalis 'Green Carpet', *P. procumbens* (Allegheny spurge).

Patient plant; see *Impatiens*

Perennial forget-me-not; see *Brunnera*

Periwinkle; see *Vinca*

Persian ivy; see *Hedera*

Pieris (py-ER-ris) **andromeda,** Native American, light to medium shade, easy, shrub.
Zones: 5 to 9
Height: 4 to 6 feet
Colors: White, pink
Characteristics: These ornamental evergreen shrubs, closely related to the rhododendron, have about eight species native to North America. The best two for the home garden are the *P. japonica* and *P. floribunda*. Both are compact in habit and produce small, delicate white flowers. The flowers of *P. japonica* form 5-inch-long, cascading clusters that look like lily of the valley gracefully hung on the shrub. These, together with dense foliage that turns bronze in the fall, make this an excellent ornamental plant. *P. japonica* 'Dorothy Wycoff' is a compact variety with pink flowers and reddish green leaves in the winter. *P. floribunda* is the hardiest of *Pieris*, native from

Virginia to Georgia. It blooms just after *P. japonica*, but its flower clusters are upright instead of cascading.
Cultural Information: Plant in well-drained, acid soil with organic matter in spring or fall. Keep the soil moist—mulch will help. Plant in a protected area away from winter winds. Pick off faded flowers to stimulate new growth. *Pieris* rarely needs fertilizing, and pruning is necessary only to maintain shape. Crown rot, fungus leaf spot, scales and mites can be problems and must be watched.
Uses: Woodland, foundation, under trees.
Recommended Varieties: Pieris japonica, P. japonica 'Dorothy Wycoff,' *P. floribunda*.

Pink summer sweet; see *Clethra*

Pink turtlehead; see *Chelone*

Plantain lily; see *Hosta,* pages 28–30

Plumbago; see *Ceratostigma*

Pachysandra *species*

Pieris japonica *'Dorothy Wycoff'*

Polygonatum odoratum
'Variegatum'

Primula × polyantha
'Dwarf Jewel'

Pulmonaria saccharata
'Mrs. Moon'

Polygonatum (po-lig-o-NA-tum) **Japanese Solomon's seal,** Native American, full to dense shade, easy, perennial.

Zones: 3 to 9
Height: 2 to 6 feet
Colors: Yellowish green to greenish white
Characteristics: A truly wonderful plant for the shaded border and for woodland and naturalized plantings, Japanese Solomon's seal has been called "the aristocrat of the woodland garden" and is grown primarily for its architectural qualities. Most of these plants are long, graceful and arching. The variegated forms are particularly striking in the shade. Japanese Solomon's seal offers deep green, 6-inch leaves, strikingly edged in yellow; the arching, 2-foot stems are rich red when they first appear. *Polygonatum odoratum* blooms with fragrant white flowers in early spring, followed by blue-black berries. *P. odoratum* 'Variegatum' is deep green edged in yellow. It has stems that are red when they first appear, and blue-black berries follow. Great Solomon's seal (*P. commutatum*) is the largest of these plants and can reach to 6 feet. A rare and choice plant that spreads rapidly and will enhance your garden from spring to early winter.
Cultural Information: Likes rich, moist soil, high in organic matter. Plant 2 to 3 feet apart in early spring. Divide for increase in early spring. Water adequately and mulch over the summer.
Uses: Shady border, woodland, cutting.
Recommended Varieties: Polygonatum odoratum, P. odoratum 'Variegatum', P. biflorum, P. commutatum.

Primrose; see *Primula*

Primula (PRIM-yew-la) **primrose,** light to full shade, easy, perennial. 🌡 ✿ ❄

Zones: 4 to 8
Height: 6 inches to 2 feet
Colors: Many
Characteristics: Primroses are appealing spring-blooming perennials, charming clustered in the woodland garden, mixed with spring bulbs, at the edges of shaded beds or under the shade of evergreens in the informal foundation planting.

  P. denticulata 'Alba' has rounded heads of dainty, pure white flowers atop 10- to 12-inch stems. *P. ×polyantha* 'Dwarf Jewel' has compact clumps of bright green leaves surrounded by clusters of brightly colored flowers. Candelabra primroses (*P. japonica*) rise 12 to 24 inches and flower in turns at the top of the stem. If given a potted primrose, enjoy it first as a houseplant and later, when the weather warms, plant it in the garden for next year's bloom. Plant tufts of primroses with yellow marsh marigolds and sheets of forget-me-nots. All will delight in spreading along the banks of a brook or throughout low, wet lands. Blue flag iris love to have their feet wet and also work well with primroses.
Cultural Information: Plant primroses in moisture-retentive soil enriched with organic matter. Sow seeds in spring or fall. They will even thrive in a bog. A winter mulch is beneficial in colder climates. Divide as they get crowded, every two to three years in late spring or summer, immediately after flowering. They grow best where spring temperatures are cool.
Uses: Woodland; edging; bank of pond, stream or bog.
Recommended Varieties: Primula denticulata 'Alba', P. × polyantha 'Dwarf Jewel', P. japonica.

Pulmonaria (pul-mo-NAY-ria) **lungwort,** light to medium shade, easy, perennial. 🌡 ✿

Zones: 3 to 8
Height: 12 inches
Colors: Blue, pink, white spotted leaves, white
Characteristics: Unlike other plants that grow foliage first and flower only after the plant is close to its mature size, *Pulmonaria* flowers early—when the leaves are only one inch long. Through the season, the leaves and the flowers bloom and grow together. The plant has increased several times in size when the flowers stop blooming; the leaves continue to grow and are 5 or more inches by summer's end.

  P. angustifolia 'Azurea' has deep green leaves with clusters of pink buds that open and change to a rich, pure blue. *P. saccharata* 'Mrs. Moon' is a real favorite because of its silvery spots on the dark green leaves. Even without flowers, it lights up a shady spot. This is an early-blooming plant and is particularly valuable in shade or partial shade as groundcovers and for naturalizing. It has dainty, drooping clusters of small blue flowers, blooming in early through late spring, and the leaves are attractive all season. 'Sissinghurst White' has white-splotched foliage and white flowers.
Cultural Information: Plant

Pulmonaria in moist, cool soil high in organic content. Plant 1 foot apart as the plants spread rapidly. Divide the plants in late summer or early spring. Division is not required, but is an excellent means of increasing clumps. Water well after dividing the plants and continue to water all fall until the ground freezes.

Uses: Groundcover, in a border, naturalizing, woodland walk.

Recommended Varieties: Pulmonaria saccharata 'Mrs. Moon', *P. saccharata* 'Sissinghurst White', *P. angustifolia* 'Azurea'.

Rhododendron (ro-do-DEN-dron) **rhododendron, azalea,** many are Native American, light, medium, full shade, easy, shrub.

Zones: 4 to 9, depending on variety

Height: Most are 4 to 6 feet; some varieties 18 inches, others to 20 feet

Colors: White, pink, lavender, mauve, yellow, orange, red, purple, bicolor

Characteristics: Botanists now classify all azaleas as *Rhododendron*. We still use the common name "azalea" to refer to the deciduous shrub. Some azaleas are evergreen, though, and some rhododendron are deciduous. Rhododendron has 10 more stamens and the leaves are often scaley. Azalea has 5 stamens, and it never has scaley leaves. Rhododendron flowers are bell shaped, whereas azalea flowers are funnel shaped. Rhododendron and azalea are among the most popular flowering plants for shade. They come in every size and color imaginable,

with so many new varieties coming out every year it is almost impossible to keep up to date. All are profuse bloomers under the right conditions, but because they need a cool, moist climate with plenty of moisture and acid soils, they cannot be grown in every zone. They are ideally suited for cultivation in the coastal northwestern states. A large part of central United States is too dry, the winters there too severe. However, breeders are busy developing varieties that are hardier for the northern and central climates, so check your nursery and catalogs.

Although they are shade-loving plants, all rhododendron need some light to produce profuse flowers. Most seem to perform best under high trees in woodland areas of light to open shade. *Rhododendron* 'Snowlady' and royal azalea *R. Schlippenbachii* will bloom in dense shade.

Choose your plant colors by the degree of shade—the reds, scarlets and purples for the brightest spots, and whites, pinks and mauves for the heavier shade. The ultimate size of your plant should be considered. Be sure to note the mature height and width of your plant so that you may plan your garden accordingly.

Cultural Information: When choosing a location for your rhododendron or azalea, select a sheltered spot away from winds, on a north-facing or west-facing slope or on the north-facing side of a building. The southern and eastern exposures usually have too much light; exposure to strong, direct sun in winter is more harmful than in the summer months. In late winter the

plants are more susceptible to wind and sun, both of which can scorch the leaves. Rhododendron and azalea prefer cool, moist, acid soil that will not be exposed for long periods to the hot summer sun. Temperate winters and moist, cloudy summers are ideal, which is why the Pacific Northwest is perfect. They will not do well in sandy soils that dry out quickly; the soil should include humus or organic matter. The soil must be acidic with a pH of 4.5 to 6.5. Mulch to keep the ground cool and keep moisture in. Peat moss or oak leaves produce acid and will help keep the pH level constant. Plant in early spring or early fall if you live in an area that does not have cold winters. Don't plant too deeply.

Pinch off faded flowers to improve bloom the following year and prune out dead, diseased or damaged branches. Cutting old branches (no more than one-third of the branches) back to the soil level will encourage new growth. Rhododendron may be propagated by seed or by stem cuttings of new growth taken in late summer and rooted in a mixture of perlite and peat moss.

Uses: Massing, slopes, hillsides, accent plant, woodland, in a border, naturalizing.

Recommended Varieties: Rhododendron carolinanum (Carolina rhododendron), *R. calendulaceum* (flame azalea), *R.* 'Klondyke', *R.* 'Snowlady', *R.* 'Vivacious', *R.* 'Pink William', *R. Schlippenbachii* (royal azalea), P.J.M. 'Elite'.

Rose of Sharon; see *Hibiscus*

Rhododendron 'Pink William'

Rhododendron 'Klondyke'

Scilla siberica
'Spring Beauty'

Tiarella cordifolia
collina

Torenia Fournieri
'Clown Mix'

Sapphire flower; see ***Browallia***

Saxifrage; see ***Bergenia***

Scilla campanulata; see ***Endymion***

Scilla siberica (SILL-a si-BIR-e-ka) **Siberian squill,** medium shade, easy, perennial
Zones: 1 to 8
Height: 4 to 6 inches
Color: Intense blue
Characteristics: This lovely, spring-flowering bulb has nodding, starlike florets ½ inch wide and green ribbonlike leaves. It blooms just after the crocus and before the daffodils, and its blooms last one to two weeks. Warm temperatures sometimes encourage it to emerge earlier. 'Spring Beauty', slightly larger than species types, is extremely easy to grow and very hardy, and because it propagates itself readily, this is an excellent bulb for naturalizing. *Scilla* is a good companion for spring bulbs. The foliage matures quickly, making this a good plant for the foreground of a planting.
Cultural Information: A most undemanding plant. Almost any soil, even without fertilizer, is tolerated, but an occasional blanket of well-rotted manure or other organic matter increases bloom. *Scilla* has normal moisture requirements. It can be divided from summer to fall but it is usually not worth the trouble —just replace with fresh bulbs.
Uses: Edging, naturalizing, rock garden.
Recommended Varieties: Scilla siberica, S. siberica 'Spring Beauty'.

Shooting star; see ***Dodecatheon***

Siberian squill; see ***Scilla***

Snowdrop; see ***Galanthus***

Solomon's seal, Japanese; see ***Polygonatum***

Spanish bluebells; see ***Endymion***

Spider plant; see ***Cleome***

Spiderwort; see ***Tradescantia***

Spirea, garden; see ***Astilbe***

Spurge, Japanese; see ***Pachysandra***

Squill, Siberian; see ***Scilla***

St.-John's-wort; see ***Hypericum***

Summersweet, pink; see ***Clethra***

Sweet alyssum; see ***Lobularia***

Sweet pepperbush; see ***Clethra***

Sweet woodruff; see ***Galium***

Tiarella (ty-a-RELL-a) **foamflower,** Native American, medium to dense shade, easy, perennial. ✳
Zones: 3 to 8
Height: 6 to 20 inches
Colors: White, light pink, rose
Characteristics: A creeping, white starflower with leaves shaped like those of maples, soft to the touch and about a foot high, this woodland flower is a member of the saxifrage family. This handsome spring bloomer is native throughout much of the eastern United States and Canada, to the Carolinas and Tennessee extending west to Michigan. It does well in almost every area of the country. It forms dense mounds 6 to 20 inches high and blooms from April to July. The leaves turn bronze in winter.
Cultural Information: Thriving in woodland acid soils, *Tiarella* spreads quickly by runners. It is a wonderful groundcover for areas where soil moisture can be retained. Add leaf mold and other organic matter annually. Propagate by seed or division.
Uses: Groundcover, rock garden, under shrubs, woodland, naturalizing.
Recommended Varieties: Tiarella cordifolia, T. cordifolia 'Purpurea'.

Toad lily; see ***Tricyrtis***

Torenia Fournieri (to-REN-ia four-nee-E-ree) **wishbone flower,** medium shade, easy, annual. ✳
Height: 8 inches
Colors: Blue, deep rose, pink, white, lavender, and bicolors with bright yellow blotch
Characteristics: Torenia was best known as a summer potted plant but today is as popular in the garden. An old-fashioned variety (and the best known) is *T. Fournieri* 'Compacta', its lavender blooms marked with dark, velvety blue and with a bright yellow blotch inside each

trumpet-shaped flower. A white variety can be found. Both of these varieties are dwarf, compact plants that offer fall color; in cool weather, the foliage turns purplish. The bloom of a new variety, 'Clown Mix', is so named because it is reminiscent of a clown's gaily painted face.

Torenia is disease resistant, long-blooming and provides pretty color in shady spots.

Cultural Information: Torenia is a rapid-growing annual that prefers rich, warm, moist soil and cool weather. It appreciates water and grows nicely along brooks and streams. Water during prolonged, hot, dry weather. If grown as a houseplant, pinching back the tips will help induce bushiness. In areas with frost, garden plants can be dug and potted for continued bloom indoors through the winter. Indoors, grow at 60°F nights, provide high humidity, diffused light and very rich soil. Keep evenly moist. Space 6 to 8 inches apart.

Uses: Groundcover, edging, in a border.

Recommended Varieties: Torenia Fournieri 'Compacta', *T.* 'Clown Mix'.

Touch-me-not; see *Impatiens*

Tradescantia (trad-ess-KAN-tia) **spiderwort,** Native American, light to medium shade, easy, perennial. 🌢

Zones: 4 to 9
Height: 1½ to 2½ feet
Colors: White, blue, pink, purple, red
Characteristics: This plant has clusters of three-petaled flowers that rise above long, narrow leaves from midsummer to early fall. The flowers close on sunny afternoons. The leaves are deep green and almost straplike. Spiderwort has the appearance of a coarse grass, as the lower portion of the leaf is wrapped around the stem. This hardy plant is easy to grow, but it has a tendency to sprawl and ramble through the garden when it is not restrained. The plant spreads by underground stems and by above-ground stems that root where their joint is in contact with the soil.

Cultural Information: Spiderwort is adaptable to many situations, from infertile soil to deep shade and boggy conditions. It does best in light to medium shade, with less blooms in darker conditions. It will tolerate any soil but should be planted 15 to 20 inches apart in moist, rich soil; if you wish to restrain the plant, it will be difficult in this soil. Native to moist soils in the eastern United States. Divide every other year, in spring, to increase and control growth. Sow seed collected in late summer. Germination takes about two weeks.

Uses: Woodland walk, in a border.

Recommended Varieties: Trandescantia virginiana, T. 'Iris Prichard', *T.* 'J. C. Weguelin', *T.* 'Purple Dome', *T.* 'Pauline', *T.* 'Snowcap', *T.* 'Red Cloud', *T. gigantea.*

Tricyrtis (try-SER-tis) **toad lily,** light to medium shade, easy, perennial.

Zones: 4 to 8
Height: 2 to 3 feet
Colors: Mauve, white
Characteristics: A very unusual and interesting-looking plant with orchidlike flowers that cluster at the leaf axils, *Tricyrtis* grows to 3 feet and forms an elegant clump of graceful, arching stems. Each flower lasts two to three weeks with some varieties lasting as much as six weeks. It blooms in early fall when few plants are flowering. *T. hirta* is the most common species with splotches of purple spots. *T. flava* is called the yellow toad lily for its lemon color. The speckled toad lily *T. macropoda* is prominently spotted.

Cultural Information: Plant in rich, moist, preferably acid soil. Make sure the soil does not dry out. Many varieties will not winter over in the North and must be brought in or mulched heavily for protection. Does not self-sow. Seeds may not be true to type. You may divide in spring or fall, but it is seldom necessary. New varieties have been introduced that will seed themselves, among them the *T.* 'Miyazaki' cultivar.

Uses: Path border, container plant (the flower has no great impact from a distance).

Recommended: Tricyrtis hirta 'Miyazaki', *T. flava, T. macropoda.*

Trillium grandiflorum (TRILL-ee-um) **white trillium,** native to eastern North America, medium to dense shade, moderate, perennial.

Zones: 4 to 9
Height: 18 to 24 inches
Colors: White, pink
Characteristics: One of the most treasured of the woodland plants, this plant should never be taken from the wild. Trillium is much more at home in forests and woodlands than in the garden. *T. grandiflorum* can be grown

Tradescantia gigantea

Tricyrtis hirta *'Miyazaki'*

Trillium grandiflorum

Trollius Ledebourii
'*Golden Queen*'

from seed and is also one of the most beautiful. It begins with shiny bronze growth and yellow buds and develops into green foliage with white flowers. It blooms April to May and is a showy native plant in the woods among shrubs and ferns. The name trillium refers to the way the plant is structured with three sepals, three leaves and three petals. The flower produces a berrylike fruit in the fall.

Cultural Information: Trillium needs the proper growing conditions of deep, rich, moist soil high in organic content and with good drainage. Soil should be neutral to slightly acid. With these conditions it will increase rapidly. Interplant with other trilliums or ferns. Mulch annually. Watch for snails and slugs. Do not cut trillium because, once the three leaves are gone, the plant loses its means of sustenance.

Uses: Woodland, informal garden, wild garden.

Recommended: Trillium grandiflorum roseum, T. grandiflorum.

Trollius (TROL-ee-us) **globeflower,** Native American, medium shade, easy, perennial.

🌡 ❀

Zones: 3 to 8
Height: 2 to 3 feet
Colors: Shades of yellow and orange
Characteristics: This plant, a member of the buttercup family, is valued for its bright, cheery yellow flowers. Species have large single or double flowers, composed of 5 to 15 showy sepals in a ball·shape that always appears as though it has never fully opened. They bloom on long stems in May and June.

The stems grow in upright clusters, creating bushy, rounded plants. The foliage remains attractive all season. They are long lived in moist conditions and naturally restrained in growth. The clumps gradually expand by sending up new shoots on the outside edge of the crown. *Trollius laxus* is native to northeastern United States and is the easiest to establish.

Cultural Information: Plant globeflower in moist soil containing plenty of compost or peat moss. It performs best in cool, moist soil and rarely performs well south of Zone 6. Remove any faded flowers to prolong the bloom period. Keep the plant well watered and never let it dry out. The plant will multiply slowly and doesn't need division to reduce crowding for five to six years. Divide plants late in summer or early in spring as an excellent means of increasing the numbers. Sow seeds in late summer by first freezing them for two days in the refrigerator, then planting outdoors. Fresh seeds germinate in six to seven weeks, whereas old seeds take two or more years. To speed up germination on old seed, plant in pots, cover with plastic wrap and freeze for a few days, then move to a warm place.

Uses: Cutting, in a border, water garden, bog garden.

Recommended Varieties: Trollius laxus, T. Ledebourii 'Golden Queen'.

Tuberous begonia; see **Begonia**

Turtlehead, pink; see **Chelone**

Viburnum (vy-BER-num) medium, full, dense shade, easy, shrub.

Zones: 3 to 8
Height: 4 to 15 feet depending on variety
Colors: White or pink flowers; some species produce berries in shades of yellow, orange, red, pink, blue, black
Characteristics: Viburnum ranks among the most ornamental and useful plants for any garden, but it is particularly useful for the shade garden because it blooms even in dense shade. This handsome shrub—some compact—is bushy with showy flowers and

Viburnum plicatum tomentosum '*Mariesii*'

attractive foliage. It has good fall coloring and many produce berries that attract birds to your garden. Some are evergreen; the deciduous varieties produce abundant white flowers in snowball forms or flat clusters. The flowers are followed by fleshy, berrylike fruits of red, yellow, blue or black. All viburnums are extremely hardy and tolerate salt spray.

Viburnum does best in medium and full shade, producing lavish blooms. In dense shade, it produces fewer blooms. All will benefit by some sun in the spring. The following varieties are the most shade tolerant: maple-leafed viburnum *(Viburnum acerifolium)*, arrowwood *(V. dentatum)*, Marie's double file viburnum *(V. plicatum tomentosum* 'Mariesii') and black haw viburnum *(V. prunifolium)*.

For light shade and one of the most glorious fragrances choose Korean spice viburnum *(V. Carlesii)*. This old-fashioned variety has been a favorite for generations. One of the hardiest varieties for the North is *V. ×Juddii*, which originated at the Arnold Arboretum in Boston in 1920. *V. ×Burkwoodii* is also hardy and fragrant.
Cultural Information: Most plants do well in almost any well-drained soil, but they especially welcome a moist, slightly acidic soil. Few of them need attention once they are established in good soil. No fertilizing is necessary. Prune only dead branches. Propagate from cuttings of new growth in late spring or early summer.
Uses: Hedge, in a border, woodland, specimen plant.
Recommended Varieties: Viburnum

acerifolium, V. dentatum, V. plicatum tomentosum 'Mariesii', *V. prunifolium, V. ×Burkwoodii, V. Carlesii.*

Vinca minor (VIN-ca MY-nor) **periwinkle or creeping myrtle,** all types of shade, easy, perennial. ◊
Zones: 4 to 9
Height: 4 to 6 inches
Colors: White, blue
Characteristics: One of the most common groundcovers for shade, *Vinca* makes a thick growth of dark evergreen, glossy leaves that remain evergreen throughout the year. Blue-, five-petaled flowers appear in April/ May, rounded and about an inch wide, and the plants often continue to flower in intervals until fall. When grown in low light there will be fewer flowers. This is one of the few groundcovers that will grow under maples. *Vinca* 'Alba' has a bright white flower. *V. minor* 'Sterling Silver' is variegated with lavender-blue flowers.
Cultural Information: Set rooted cuttings or divisions in rich, moist, well-drained soil 12 to 18 inches apart in spring. Prepare the soil before planting by adding organic matter and water well until plants are established. If planted in too much sun, foliage will yellow. To keep foliage thick and a rich green, water and feed with lawn fertilizer during warm months. To propagate, divide old plants in spring or by rooted stem cuttings at any time in spring or fall.
Uses: Under trees, path border, slopes, under large bulbs, trailing wall, edging, container plant.
Recommended Varieties: Vinca minor 'Alba', *V. minor* 'Bowles'.

Viola (VIE-o-la) **violet,** light to full shade, easy, annual and perennial. ◊ ❀ ✳
Zones: 3 to 10, depending on variety
Height: 4 to 12 inches
Colors: Blue, purple, white, yellow
Characteristics: One of the most charming and romantic of flowers, violets include annual and perennial species, altogether some 500 species. Most members of the violet family are spring-blooming woodland perennials. The annual, large-flowered varieties are usually referred to as pansies. Most species are low growing and make good groundcovers, or can fill in the bare spots beneath shrubs. Violets spread fairly rapidly by seeding themselves or by creeping roots.

The true violets are perennials and include the sweet violet *(Viola odorata)*, and the tufted violet *(V. cornuta)*. The sweet violet has been grown for centuries. It was the sweet violet that Napoleon gave Josephine every year on their anniversary, and the sweet violet has been the subject of many a poem.

Vinca minor

Viola cornuta 'Princess Blue'

Viola tricolor

Intensely fragrant, it was a source of oils for the perfume industry for many years. 'Czar' and 'Lady Hume Campbell', a double-flowering variety, are both nice.

V. cornuta is a vigorous grower and makes an excellent ground-cover. *V. cornuta* 'Princess Blue', an exceptional Burpee breeding triumph, lavishly produces its velvet, violet-blue, 1-inch flowers from spring through midsummer and then again in fall. It's easy to grow from seed and blooms in about 70 days when started indoors.

The bird's-foot violet *(V. pedata)* is one of the loveliest violets and one of my favorites. It's also a Native American seen in the eastern United States to Minnesota. Make sure you have good drainage for this one.

The most commonly known and loved Johnny-jump-up *(V. tricolor)* is usually called the pansy. There are many kinds of pansies, all of which can be grown in partial or medium shade and give profuse bloom all summer long. Johnny-jump-up is one of the smaller plants with little flowers that bloom from early spring to frost, so bright they seem to jump up at you. *V. tricolor* 'Imperial Blue' is an AAS winner with the bluest, largest flowers.

Cultural Information: Violets like well-drained, humus-rich soil that is slightly acid. Sweet violets require a moist soil and Labrador violets tolerate drier conditions. They grow best where they receive at least several hours of unfiltered sun. In late summer, early fall or after the last frost in spring, plant rooted divisions and water daily until new foliage appears, then keep moist. Spreads rapidly by seeding itself, by surface runners and by creeping roots. They prefer cooler weather and may die back in summer to return in fall; breeders are working to develop heat-tolerant varieties.

Pansies will grow in any good garden soil but do best when supplemented with organic matter. Remove faded flowers and seed pods to keep plants blooming and in a more compact growing state. Cut back over the summer when they become "leggy" to induce more flowers and a neater habit. In southern climates with a long growing season, clumps can be divided. All parts of the pansy are poisonous. Space plants 6 inches apart.

Uses: Container plant, window box, woodland, naturalizing.

Recommended Varieties: Viola ordorata, V. cornuta 'Princess Blue', *V. tricolor, V.×Wittrockiana* 'Jolly Joker', *V. ×Wittrockiana* 'Padparadja', *V. ×Wittrockiana* 'Max immarina', Majestic Giant Hybrids.

Violet; see ***Viola***

Violet, dog-tooth; see ***Erythronium***

Virginia bluebells; see ***Mertensia***

Wax begonia; see ***Begonia***

White trillium; see ***Trillium***

Wild ginger; see ***Asarum***

Wintercreeper; see ***Euonymus***

Wishbone flower; see ***Torenia***

Witch hazel; see ***Hamamelis***

Wood hyacinth; see ***Endymion***

Woodruff, sweet; see ***Galium***

Yellow corydalis; see ***Corydalis***

PESTS AND DISEASES

One of the best things about shade gardening is that the majority of pests rarely attack the shade plants in a serious way. The shadier the garden, the fewer aphids, caterpillars and scale insects you will see. When you do see them they are usually in the areas that receive the most sun. The most common garden pests for the shade garden are slugs, snails and root weevils. Shade gardeners still get visits from the other common pests as well as diseases, and there are some precautions you can take to minimize these problems.

DISEASE PREVENTION

Prevention is always the best medicine, whether it be for ourselves or for our plants in the garden. Just as is the case with a healthy person, a healthy plant is better able to ward off an attack. But things go wrong even in the best-cared-for gardens and disease can strike even the healthiest of plants. Do everything you can to prevent pests and diseases, be alert for early detection and act swiftly with the right treatment.

There are several things you can do to try to prevent trouble before it starts in order to keep your garden healthy:

1. *GROW DISEASE-RESISTANT VARIETIES*. Breeders are constantly coming up with new varieties of plants every year that resist the diseases commonly associated with that variety. If your area is prone to certain diseases, look for varieties that are resistant to them. Different plants are susceptible to different diseases, and a disease is more easily contained if you grow several varieties rather than the same variety. Once one plant is infected, the disease will spread among plants of the same variety.

2. *PREPARE YOUR GROUND THOROUGHLY*. A sturdy plant that has the benefit of good soil with plenty of nutrients, ample water and no weeds will have a greater chance of recovery from a pest or disease attack than a weak plant that lacks such support.

3. *DON'T WATER AT NIGHT, AND DON'T WORK IN WET GARDENS*. Watering in the evening doesn't give plant foliage enough time to dry off, and this can promote disease. Working among wet plants also spreads disease more easily.

4. *DESTROY DISEASED PLANTS*. Burn a diseased plant or put it in a separate container to be thrown away. Never put a diseased plant on the compost pile as it will spread infection.

5. *KEEP YOUR GARDEN CLEAN*. Do not leave dead flowers, leaves or other garden debris out. Cut perennials down after their foliage has died. Garden debris makes a perfect home for insects and slugs.

6. *CHOOSE YOUR PLANTS WISELY*. Do not buy soft bulbs or leggy bedding plants. Check plants carefully for any wilted leaves or sickly looking areas.

7. *INSPECT PLANTS REGULARLY*. Check your plants on a regular basis for any signs of trouble, and then act quickly when you spot them.

8. *SPACING*. Proper spacing allows good air circulation and helps prevent disease.

COMMON PESTS OF THE SHADE GARDEN

Slug

Snail

SLUGS: Slugs and snails are the most common pests in the shade garden. This is true for the majority of the country, the only exceptions being the deserts and the prairies. Slugs can be brown, black, gray or reddish tan, depending on the area of the country that you live in, but they all have the same voracious appetite. Slugs are not insects but are classified as mollusks. Slugs cause serious damage to a great variety of plants.

Slugs feed at night when conditions are cooler and damp. On damp, misty or overcast days you may see them feeding during the day. They crawl along leaving a conspicuous silvery slime wherever they go. They chew irregular holes in leaves and hide under leaves, mulch or rocks during the day. Acid soils are particularly favorable to slugs.

Treatment: Put a ring of wood ashes, lime, diatomaceous earth or coarse sand around the base of affected plants. This will prevent the slugs from crawling up the plant as they dislike going over scratchy surfaces. You can purchase diatomaceous material from Ringers. These substances will need to be sprinkled rather frequently during periods of wet weather.

A shallow container of beer set with the rim at soil surface level is an old favorite for attracting slugs and drowning them. Another method is to use the skin of half of an orange, propped up by a small stone. The slug will use it for shelter and shade during the day. All you have to do is collect the slugs on a regular basis and destroy them.

Slugs lay white, semitransparent eggs in the soil and other damp locations. Watch for and destroy them. There is also a slug bait called "metaldehyde," but it is always preferable to use natural methods and resort to chemicals only as a last resort. In the case of slugs, you'll find that chemical control will probably never be necessary. A watchful eye and a collection can at dusk are the best methods.

SNAILS: Snails differ from slugs in that they have a hard shell into which they can retreat from danger or when they sleep. The common garden variety is usually brown-shelled with black markings. They, too, move by crawling, leave the silvery slime trail and feed at night. Snails are notorious along the California coast, where they are worse pests than slugs. The droughts in the West have reduced some populations, but their shells give them protection. Snails do serious damage to almost any kind of plant, but plants in the seedling stage are the preferred choice. Decaying vegetable matter is also eaten.

Treatment: Same as for slugs. Check under evergreen groundcovers such as English ivy and pachysandra for snail colonies over the winter. This is a good time to collect and destroy them. When you hand-collect snails, put them in a pail with a strong solution of salty water.

WEEVILS: One of the more serious of the shade garden pests, weevils are particularly fond of a large number of shade plants such as primrose, rhododendron, azalea, *Pieris*, *Bergenia*, coralbells and viburnum. The weevils that attack these plants are usually either the black vine weevil or the strawberry root weevil. The adults eat the foliage and the grubs attack the roots. The adult leaves an oddly notched mark on the outside edges of the leaves. Another sign of weevils is if the entire shrub or plant goes limp and brown.

Treatment: Adult weevils hide in the soil during the day, so remove accumulations of leaves and other plant debris.

To eradicate the larvae, the only method known to work is, unfortunately, chemical. Apply 5 percent chlordane dust or diazinon to the soil, 1 pound to 200 square feet. Alternatively, soak the soil beneath and directly around the plant with any contact poison (malathion, for example). Repeat the application every several weeks from spring to fall. This soaking will save most of the plants.

JAPANESE BEETLES: A major pest east of the Mississippi but rapidly making its way west, the Japanese beetle is a coppery green beetle that emerges from the ground in early summer and feeds on flowers and foliage of many different kinds of plants. When they finish with a leaf there is almost nothing left of it except its mere vein of an outline. After 30 to 40 days of life as adults, they lay their eggs in the soil. The larvae hatch and eat the roots of plants and grass for several months before burrowing themselves deeper in the ground for winter. They emerge again the following year and repeat the cycle.

Treatment: Beetle traps are available that lure beetles with a natural sex attractant. The beetles fly or crawl into the trap and can't get out. Another good trap is a can of water with a thin film of oil on the water surface. Flick the slow-moving beetles into the can, and they won't be able to fly out.

Safer Grub Killer is a powder that contains bacterial spores (*Bacillus popillae*, milky spore disease) toxic only to Japanese beetles and other grubs. It will not harm birds or pets, and is safe to handle.

APHIDS: Aphids are small insects that feed by sucking the sap from plants, causing stunted growth, distorted leaves and other deformities. They secrete a sweet, sticky liquid substance called "honeydew" and this attracts ants, which feed on it. If you see ants around your plants, you probably have aphids. This sticky substance also forms a medium on which a mold fungus grows and can disfigure plants.

Treatment: Mix two tablespoons of liquid dishwashing detergent per gallon of water and spray on the plant.

NEMATODES: Nematodes are everywhere. Microscopic in size and often invisible to the naked eye, they measure only 1/50 to ⅛ inch and are wormlike creatures. They stunt plant growth by damaging the roots and causing the leaves of the plant to yellow.

Few pests are able to increase so rapidly or cause so much serious damage in such a short period of time. Gardeners know of the existence of nematodes only by the damage they do. Check your roots for lobes or knots. If you suspect nematodes, the best thing to do is to send a soil sample to your state agricultural lab for testing. This is inexpensive and well worth the trouble to follow up with a telephone call.

Treatment: Increase the organic content of your soil so as to attract beneficial creatures to fight these harmful ones. French marigolds can be planted as a deterrant because they attract the beneficial nematodes that ward off the destructive ones.

Aphids

COMMON DISEASES OF THE SHADE GARDEN

MILDEW: Mildew and powdery mildew are fungi that grow on the surface of the plant. They form a white, felty coat on leaves and stems. All powdery mildews are parasitic. They obtain their nourishment through tiny suckers. Powdery mildews thrive when the atmosphere is humid but not during rainy weather. Cool nights following warm days feed the growth of these fungi. When plants are crowded together or there are other factors limiting air circulation, the mildews flourish.

Treatment: Space out your plants to provide good air circulation, to help avoid damp conditions. Affected plants may be in too much shade. Try moving them to an area with a bit more light. Avoid overhead watering, especially late in the day when water on the foliage doesn't have a chance to dry.

CHLOROSIS: This is a yellowing of leaves—while veins remain green, the leaves turn pale and the tips brown. Rhododendron, azalea and hydrangea are particularly susceptible to this. This condition is usually caused by a deficiency of iron. Iron can be depleted by root injury, by cultivation, by allowing the soil to become too dry, by sandy soil with insufficient organic matter or by too much lime in the soil leached from nearby concrete foundations.

Treatment: Improvement of the soil is the only permanent solution. Use plenty of organic matter and include a 2- to 3-inch layer of mulch.

LEAF SPOT: This condition is identified by irregular water-soaked spots with yellow or translucent borders usually caused by fungus diseases or bacterial diseases. It appears on lower or inside leaves of densely crowded foliage and on English ivy. Stem infections could result in reduction of growth.

Treatment: Improve ventilation and pick and destroy infected leaves. Avoid overhead watering or splashing when watering, as this is how the disease is transmitted.

Japanese beetle

GARDENERS' MOST-ASKED QUESTIONS

Q: Don't most plants grow better in the sun?
A: Not necessarily. Shade plants have evolved to thrive in the shade, and some can burn if exposed to too much light. It's always better to choose an appropriate plant for the space you have in mind rather than choose the plant first and then hunt for a location. Plants have adapted to specific environments over thousands of years, and although small adjustments can be made, in general they will perform best in those environmental conditions.

Q: I've heard that plants will grow taller in the shade. Why?
A: Although it depends on the plant, often the same plant variety will grow taller when planted in the shade than in the sun. Plants need light to manufacture their food and will actually stretch for the light if they are in the shade.

Q: Is bloom affected by the shade?
A: Many plants won't bloom if they do not receive enough light,

unless they are naturally shade tolerant. Plants use sunlight to make food for themselves. When they don't get enough sun, or if they don't have enough nutrients from the soil or fertilizer, they will first stop producing fruits, then flowers, then stop growing, and finally die. In order to stay alive, they will stop doing whatever takes the most energy.

Q: Are shade plants lower maintenance?
A: Shade plants tend to require less maintenance because fewer weeds grow in the shade and there are fewer insect problems. Slugs, however, may be worse in the shade, and air circulation can be worse, giving some disease problems a headstart.

Q: Nothing grows under my maple tree. What can I do?
A: There are probably two problems with the location: lots of shade and lots of root competition. Maples provide dense shade, and they have shallow root systems that can take the nutrients and water from the soil

before a newly planted plant has a chance to get established. Avoid planting slow-to-establish plants under maples; climbing hydrangea and *Schrizophragma* vines are just such plants. *Vinca minor*, on the other hand, usually grows well under maples.

Q: Plants don't grow under my black walnut tree. Is it too shady?
A: Chances are that plants die under your black walnut because of the toxins that exist in the leaves, roots and fruits of this tree. Too little long-term research has been done on this subject for us to be able to give you sure-fire recommendations, so you will have to do a little experimenting of your own to determine what will grow there.

Q: What is the difference between "shade tolerant" and "shade loving"?
A: Some plants perform best in the sun but will also perform in shade. These plants prefer sun, but are "shade tolerant." A "shade-loving" plant is one that actually prefers a degree of

shade to full sun. In the Burpee catalog, we try to list all the conditions under which plants will grow, in order of preference.

Q: *Do plants grow more slowly in the shade? My daffodils in shade come out later than the same variety planted in sun.*
A: In spring the ground takes longer to heat up in the shade because the sun doesn't hit it directly for as long. Most spring-flowering plants will emerge later in the shade. They do not always grow more slowly throughout the season, however. The rate of growth depends on the variety and its adaptation to shady locations.

Q: *Why are shady areas so often more informal looking than sunny garden areas? Why do there seem to be more native plants?*
A: Shade-loving plants tend to be less showy than sun-loving, garden plants. Many of the best shade plants are found in our native woodlands, areas that are informal by definition. These plants—including ferns, native bulbs such as *Erythronium*, perennials such as *Tiarella* and *Mertensia*, and native shrubs such as viburnum and azalea species—grow better in the shade than many introduced species because they are being grown in conditions similar to those of their native environments. Obviously, not all parts of this country have the same conditions, but if you choose plants that grow naturally in conditions sim-

ilar to those in your garden, those plants can be expected to thrive for you.

Q: *What is the connection between moisture and shade?*
A: Most shady locations tend to have higher moisture content than sunny locations, as the vegetation shading the area protects much of the moisture from evaporation. Most shade-loving plants, therefore, are moisture-loving plants. Some can adapt to brighter locations as long as adequate moisture is provided. When the shade is provided by a building or other nonvegetal structure, some shade-loving plants will require extra moisture because rain is unable to reach the plants due to the obstruction of the building.

Q: *Should one consider color when planning a shade garden more than one would for a sunny garden?*
A: Color considerations are neither more nor less important in shade gardening than in sun gardening, but the approach to choosing color is more subtle. Softer, cooler colors, such as pinks, lavenders, blues, whites and silvers, look better in shade than bright colors. Foliage color can be more important in shade gardening, and some designs for shade will include only foliage plants. Choose foliage in more interesting colors and textures, such as the bluish leaves on 'Krossa Regal' hosta and the silvery fronds of Japanese painted fern.

Q: *Are there any plants that should be grown in shade in one geographical region and in sun in another?*
A: Some plants not tolerant of very warm weather are best grown in partial shade when grown in the South. It is best to check with your local Cooperative Extension Service if you are in doubt, for advice on whether specific plants perform well in your area. You can always experiment, especially in borderline cases!

Q: *Why are there so few narrow-leafed shade plants?*
A: Shade plants tend to have broader or larger leaves than full-sun plants. Broader leaves provide more surface area for these plants to catch and use what sunlight they can.

Q: *I live in the city and have a shady balcony. What can I plant in containers?*
A: You can try *Caladium*, impatiens, begonias, clematis (give the vine something for it to climb), *Achimenes*, large-leafed tropical houseplants, coleus and even ferns.

Please call or write for a free Burpee catalog:

W. Atlee Burpee & Company
300 Park Avenue
Warminster, PA 18974

215-674-9633

THE USDA PLANT HARDINESS MAP OF THE UNITED STATES

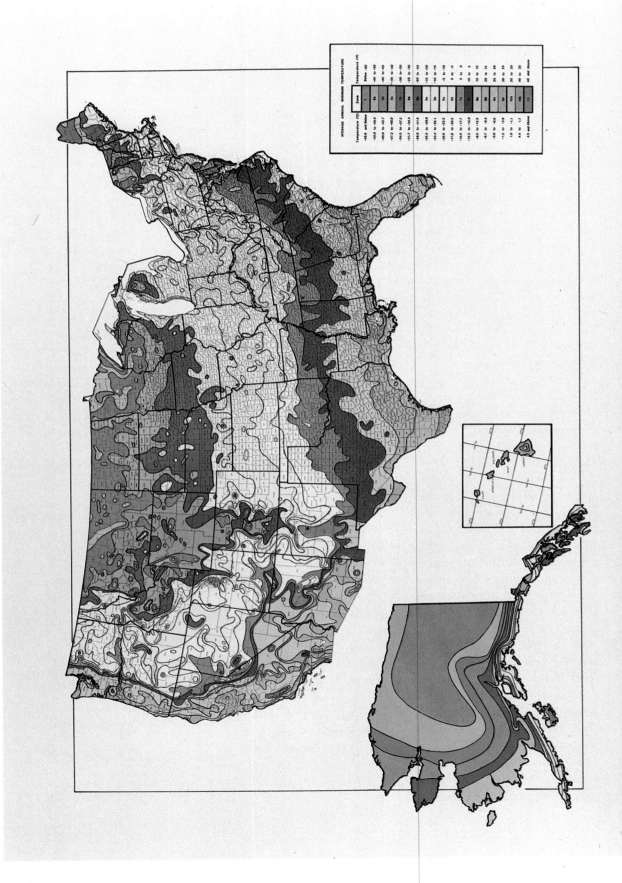

INDEX

Window
gardens

You'll be the toast of the neighborhood when you dress up your windows with flower-filled window boxes. These small gardens are a dream come true for time-pressured gardeners. Upkeep is easy—all it takes is watering, fertilizing, and pinching.

by Julie A. Martens

Complementary Colors

A simple pine window box painted and planted in colors that complement your home's exterior can set your house apart. Here, tall salmon-colored salvia and apricot dahlias provide a peach backdrop for blue-flowered Sky Blue pansies, petunias, and trailing swan river daisy. Peaches and Cream verbena and lantana add the final touches to this peach of a window garden.

PHOTOGRAPHS: ERIC ROTH. REGIONAL EDITOR: ESTELLE BOND GURALNICK. PLANTING DESIGN: LOU AND PAT ZUMSTEIN

Window
gardens

Shade-Tolerant Blooms

Rosebud impatiens, above, *brighten even the shadiest side of a house. Like all impatiens, these double-flowered beauties need a lot to drink, so water containers daily once plants start blooming. Other bloomers that will brighten shady corners include single-flowered impatiens, browallia, and tuberous begonias.*

Window Box Banquet

Even a window box can be a gourmet garden when you choose all edible plants. Alpine strawberries, Boston lettuce, English thyme, curry, mint, Johnny-jump-ups, nasturtiums, and scented geraniums are just some of the harvest-fresh flavors in this garden, right. A stencil done in acrylics personalizes the box.

In the Pink

Pink geraniums and pink impatiens make perfect planting partners for a window box that's in a sometimes sunny, sometimes shady spot, below. To add some trailing interest, there's nothing like easy-to-find variegated Vinca major. For a blooming vine, try nierembergia, sweet alyssum, Zinnia angustifolia, or sanvitalia.

Window
gardens

Bulb Bonanza

What better way to announce spring's arrival than with your favorite bulbs in a window garden? This display works best when you plant bulbs in a container that fits inside the window box. You can either force bulbs in fall or buy ready-to-bloom bulbs in spring. In this garden, above, *drifts of narcissus, Red Riding Hood tulips with striped leaves, and grape hyacinths welcome spring.*

Bouquet-Filled Box

Let your imagination run wild when choosing flowers for a window garden, and the result will be simply charming. Left, *cheery pansy faces play peekaboo with roses, geraniums, and rosebud impatiens in a combination that's suitable for any window. To keep the flower show strong throughout the summer, remove spent blossoms to encourage more blooms.*

Pageantry in Purple

Planting a window garden in shades of a single hue turns a favorite color into a blooming extravaganza. Purple is the flower color of choice for this blue-shuttered window, below. *Petunias and Victoria Blue salvia create a striking backdrop for trailing swan river daisy and lobelia. Silver lace artemisia and verbena brighten the blue tones.*

Window
gardens

Nostalgic Nosegays

*Capture the floral profusion of an
old-fashioned cottage garden with a window
box that's stuffed with flowers. Daisies,
impatiens, petunias, pansies, swan river daisy,
lobelia, and vinca put on a nonstop floral show
when the garden gets at least half a day of sun.
If your window garden faces south, line the
inside of the box with a sheet of plastic foam
before filling it with soil. The foam acts as an
insulator and reduces soil temperatures.*

Buying information, page 170

How to plant a window garden

*To add flowery focal points to your windows, you'll need a container, soil, plants, and only a small amount of
time. If you're baffled about which flowers will look good together, just look at a color wheel. Colors opposite
each other make an eye-catching display every time.*

1. **In a window garden,** *plants' root
systems are squeezed into a small space.
Using the right soil mix is crucial. Sunshine
mix, above, is a perfect choice; it has
Canadian sphagnum peat moss, a wetting
agent, and a fertilizer. Look for Sunshine
mixes at lawn and garden centers.*

2. **Choose healthy plants** *from a
reputable nursery. If you want a window
garden that's immediately filled with
bursting blooms, buy plants in 4-inch pots.
Remember to place taller plants toward the
back and center of the container and
trailing plants toward the front and sides.*

3. **Water the window garden**
*thoroughly after planting. Frequent
watering is critical for continuous blooms.
Check containers daily in spring and twice
daily in summer. To display your finished
window garden, mount the container with
the top edge just below the windowsill.* 🏠